# Miracle Mountain

## WHERE VOLUNTEERS
## LEFT THEIR MARK

## JAY WALSH

Ps. 127:1

ABWE PUBLISHING®

HARRISBURG, PA

MIRACLE MOUNTAIN
Copyright © 1998 by ABWE Publishing
Harrisburg, PA 17105

Library of Congress Cataloging-in-Publication Data
  (Application Pending)
Walsh, D. Jay, 1932–
  Miracle Mountain: Where Volunteers Left Their Mark
  Jay Walsh
  Non-Fiction
  ISBN: 1-888796-15-4 (Trade Paper)

Printed in the United States of America.

# DEDICATION

This volume is dedicated to all the wonderful volunteers who made the "miracle on the hill" happen, and especially to Raymond Gerow of Schoolcraft, Michigan, who suffered permanent injury to his back when the tractor compactor he was driving rolled over the edge of a high embankment, throwing him onto jagged rocks.

*Raymond Gerow*

# ACKNOWLEDGEMENTS

I am greatly indebted to **Kristen Stagg** for her painstaking work in retyping, proofreading, and editing my manuscript. Her God-given talent as a writer gives her the ability to identify my many mistakes. Ouch! Thank you, Kristen.

**Wendell Kempton, William Pierson, Ralph Gruenberg,** and my wife, **Eleanor** (my greatest support and encourager), were kind enough to read the manuscript and offer their suggestions to improve the final draft.

My publisher, **Jeannie Lockerbie Stephenson,** kept nudging me to write this historical account. A faithful backer and supporter, she also used her valuable time to read the manuscript and offer many helpful suggestions. Thank you, Jeannie.

—*Jay Walsh*

*On the following pages, volunteers' names appear in the order that they were signed into the register, not necessarily the chronological order in which individuals worked. We apologize for names of volunteers that were omitted because the individuals did not sign the register, as well as for any misspellings that may have occurred.*

Cherith Pierson  Jessica Petrone  Daniel Baker  Bob Hammaker  Roger Sprague  Jeni Gentzler  Sharon Hammaker  Larry Book  Jeff Sprague

Architect's rendering of the proposed ABWE headquarters in Harrisburg, Pa.

*Gary Helsel   Barbara Helsel   Susie Baker   Bob Garnham   Bill Parsons   Sam Weirouch   Tim Sorber   Tom Enman   John Buchanan*

# FOREWORD

This book tells the miraculous story of how, in 1993, God directed the leadership of the Association of Baptists for World Evangelism, Inc. (ABWE) to move the mission's headquarters from the expensive Cherry Hill, New Jersey, area to its present location near Harrisburg, Pennsylvania. This book stands as a record of that extraordinary event.

To obtain the facts regarding the decision to relocate, I relied heavily upon the official minutes of the mission, Ralph Gruenberg's *Volunteer Information Bulletins,* and the special presidential releases to ABWE board members and the mission family from 1989–1993.

The reader will benefit from the three major themes permeating these pages. The first centers around spiritual leadership. Throughout the book you will understand the heart of the president as he sincerely desires to know God's perfect will. After much prayer, and on a step-by-step basis, God's will was made known. You will also see Wendell W. Kempton's concern for the staff during a major upheaval in their lives.

Secondly, the "miracle on the hill" could not have happened without generous donors. These special people understand the words of our Lord when He said, "It is more blessed to give than to receive" (Acts 20:35).

Lastly, you will find in this book the wonderful spirit of volunteerism. As was true when the Israelites rebuilt the walls of Jerusalem in Nehemiah's day, we saw a similar spirit of unselfish teamwork. God sent His special servants—volunteers—to accomplish a huge building program that saved the mission more than $2 million. May the reading of this book kindle a desire in your heart to serve the Lord as a volunteer.

—*Jay Walsh*

Tammy Cohick  Sandra Lyons  Bob Verzella  Phil Verzella  Tony Verzella  Tom McCully  Larry Inskeep  Lee Goddard  Paul Henry, Jr.

# TABLE OF CONTENTS

1. "Tom Sawyer" teen work crew.  2. Jay and his harmonica.  3. Some of the 9,000 ft. of painted fence.  4. Filipino volunteers.  5. Don Phelps singing.  6. Shirt and cap given to volunteers.

*Jay Lee  Kee Park  Won Lee  Sung Soo Byun  Kwang Kim  J. Robert Marsh  Laura Marsh  Robert G. Marsh  Steve McNeely*

# Volunteers:
# God's Special Servants

Volunteer: "A person who chooses freely to enter into any transaction with no promise of compensation."
—Webster

By anyone's reckoning, constructing 30,500 square feet of new office space to connect two existing buildings (that needed remodeling) on the side of a mountain, would definitely require a good architect and a great engineer. To accomplish such a formidable task with volunteer labor would be almost unthinkable. But when Wendell W. Kempton, visionary president of ABWE (Association of Baptists for World Evangelism, Inc.), asked pastor and engineer Ralph Gruenberg to become the project manager, he also had the courage to suggest that the work be done by volunteers. "After all," President Kempton reasoned, "churches send volunteers all over the world to help on foreign projects. Why can't volunteers help us in Harrisburg? They won't need visas or shots, and they won't have to learn a new language."

A few savvy business people expressed doubts about the plan to use volunteers; and rightly so, from their viewpoint. But the ABWE team was determined, sensing God's approval. A letter of challenge was prepared by Wendell and sent to 8,000 pastors. The response was overwhelming. From the time of groundbreaking in August 1992 until the new office was dedicated in September 1993, more than 1,100 people from 27 states and several foreign countries donated their time and talents. Those special servants of God made the "miracle on the hill" possible. The miracle was not the new office building, but those wonderful people who made it happen.

Who were the volunteers? Among those who came were an airport manager, a private detective, a flight engineer, and a glass etcher. Men and women, teenagers and senior citizens, rich and poor, professionals and laymen, pastors and missionaries volunteered, including the president and staff of ABWE. Each one played an important role.

What did they do? The project involved surveying; operating heavy equipment; digging trenches; blasting dynamite; shoveling sand and gravel; pouring concrete; lifting timbers and steel; pounding nails; running miles of electric, computer, and telephone wire; installing plumbing, heating, and air-conditioning; and painting walls. Week after week the right people with the right skills for that week's tasks arrived. Only the Lord could have brought it all together, prompting people to volunteer. The project approximated remodeling two houses, building 15 more, and paving a half-mile of roadway and a huge parking lot: the equivalent of a small subdivision.

Volunteers not only donated their time to work on the project, they made other sacrifices as well. Many gave up vacations, working 8- to 12-hour days, six days a week and most holidays; they also paid for their travel, food, and lodging. They are special people who love their Savior and wanted to serve Him in their unique ways. They stood shoulder to shoulder performing the jobs assigned to them. They worked hard through all kinds of weather. Once winter set in, the cold weather hardly ever let up. Snowfalls, some unusually heavy,

*Justin Wouwode  Jeff Vickman  Bonnie Vickman  Wyman Ritchie  Bob Beikert  Grace Beikert  Joshua Brown  Ralph Baker  Bill Pollard*

were frequent. When all contractors in the area were shut down, the ABWE volunteers insisted on working. Sometimes 50 mph winds accompanied heavy rains and sleet, resulting in horrific mud that was terrible to walk in, much less to work in. Yet the volunteers persevered.

Shortly into the project a daily routine was established in order to accomplish the maximum amount of work within a given week. The day started at 6:30 a.m. with devotions (often involving insights on missions), testimonies, and prayer. Those were precious times: times when some made significant spiritual decisions, times of laughter and of tears, times of bonding in the Lord. Ralph's observation is poignant, "One morning a bulldozer operator from New York, an electrician from Ontario, Canada, a black teenager from western New York, a pastor from Pennsylvania, a construction worker from Ohio, a one-armed carpenter from Michigan, a cook from Connecticut, and many others were sitting around the room. We sat in silence as Don Phelps, director of music at Grace Baptist Church of Chattanooga, Tennessee, sang *A Mighty Fortress Is Our God* a cappella. As I glanced around, there was hardly a dry eye in the place. Most of those faces were new, and yet a camaraderie was already developing. We all knew the same God. He had handpicked each of us to carry out His purpose on the hill."

Morning and afternoon coffee breaks provided sugar highs, but mealtimes were really special. Women volunteers, sharing their own recipes, prepared nourishing lunches and suppers. After dinner some of the volunteers, having already put in eight hours of hard work, continued to work into the night. One of them stated, "We can only be here for a few days, so we need to make sure our time counts to the max." No commercial contractor would ever get those kind of extra hours out of highly paid employees, but the volunteers at ABWE delighted in putting in the extra effort.

*Carl Dickerson  Dana Steele  Donald Brown  Steven Brown  Stephanie Aittama  Jennifer Lewis  Jessica Lewis  Karen Goodridge*

The hardest part came at the end of the week when we said good-bye to those who had to leave. They shared testimonies, shed tears, and wore their new caps and T-shirts, thank-you gifts from ABWE which read: I Was A Part Of The Miracle At Harrisburg. At the end of the week volunteers left for home, exhausted but spiritually satisfied.

The volunteers counted spiritual growth one of the chief benefits of the project. One volunteer expressed it this way, "I consider my time on the hill to be one of the highlights of my life. I have worked on many projects, but never have I sensed the fellowship of the Spirit more than my time there."

Apart from the spiritual impact, which was most important, the volunteers saved ABWE more than $2 million in labor and material costs, money the mission didn't have in the bank at the time. What an awesome God we serve!

Moving the ABWE headquarters after 20 years in Cherry Hill, New Jersey, was a huge step of corporate faith. How the idea originated and came to fruition is a wonderful story in itself, a story of how ABWE's president, Wendell Kempton, the board, and the staff were sensitive to God's perfect will.

1. Aerial view of land-locked Cherry Hill around ABWE. 2. ABWE headquarters: 1720 Springdale Rd., Cherry Hill, New Jersey. 3. Cramped offices in Cherry Hill.

# Feeling the Pinch

O ver a 20-year period, ABWE's headquarters in Cherry Hill, New Jersey, once a rural setting, had become one big suburban gridlock. That, and the simple fact that the mission outgrew the property, with no scope to enlarge, sparked the idea of relocating. The last straw: Cherry Hill township would not allow ABWE even one more parking space.

Should God now signal a move of the headquarters, it would be the third in ABWE's 65-year history. ABWE started in 1927 in the Doane home in Watch Hill, Rhode Island. Mrs. Marguerite Doane and Mrs. Lucy Peabody provided direction for the fledgling mission and much of the support for its five missionaries in the Philippines. In 1932 a business office was opened in the Schaff Building in downtown Philadelphia. Three years later, Mrs. Peabody resigned as president and Dr. Harold T. Commons, "a promising young man," assumed the presidency over 18 missionaries. In 1971 ABWE moved to Cherry Hill, New Jersey. By that time the mission had grown to more than 350 missionaries in 11 countries. Harold Commons retired and Rev. Wendell W. Kempton became ABWE's third president.

In his annual report for the April 1989 board meetings, Wendell Kempton enumerated 10 goals for the mission. Goal number nine was, "To develop a master plan for the ABWE property and building that will care for the home office until the year 2000 and beyond." At that time he was referring to the 5.1 acres the mission owned in Cherry Hill.

Wendell's vision and concern for the future growth of the mission weighed heavily on his mind. He felt keenly the need to provide adequate space for the expanding staff, and for new services for the ABWE constituency. He shared his burden with the President's Administrative Committee (PAC). Their discussions centered around how to maximize use of the existing property.

But serious questions that arose during the following three months changed their focus. The Finance Committee minutes of July 25, 1990, under the title *ABWE Relocation*, recorded: "The mission is seriously considering a move of the headquarters office. This is primarily due to the high cost of living in South Jersey in the areas of car insurance, property taxes, and the high cost of purchasing homes. A preliminary study has been made by the committee of the Harrisburg, Pennsylvania, vicinity and other areas simply to compare prices."

Other factors influenced the decision to consider moving. Several of ABWE's administrators would soon retire and their replacements would need to purchase homes. Six other mission organizations had already moved out of the region for economic reasons. Wendell shared these concerns with the board and asked for their prayers. The year 1990 ended with a strong moving mentality!

*Melinda Bantle  Jay VanHeukelum  Philip Brown  Edward Lehman  Maryhelen Lehman  Scott Leer  Lance Helsel  Michelle Hammaker*

# Capitol View Manor

### Executive Estate / Corporate Retreat

**E**njoy the change of seasons from the courtyard patio which is accessable from many rooms.

**S**ituated on a private lane in a country setting, just minutes from I-83 and the Pennsylvania Turnpike, is this three year old custom built home featuring approximately 8,000 sq. ft. of living space. Highlights of the home include a striking foyer with a circular staircase which ascends to an area that is perfect for entertaining, a billards room and a den with custom poplar accents, a total of 8 bedrooms with an impressive master bedroom suite complete with a sitting room, a wet bar and a whirlpool spa. Additional features include 2 modern kitchens, 5 fireplaces, a formal living room with hardwood flooring, a formal dining room with twin built in china closets and much, much more...

**A** guest house with a shop can be varied in it's uses.

**H**orse lovers will appreciate the over 150 acres of woods and pasture complete with 2 barns

**T**his 4,000 sq.ft. ranch home includes 5 bedrooms and 2 baths

1. Bob Hughes, real estate agent for Jack Gaughen Realtors, who worked with ABWE.
2., 3. The brochure enumerating the benefits of Capitol View Manor.

*Linda Nauta   Karl Haefka   David Ruffer   Randon Riegsecker   Wes Stowell   Ruth Kempton   Samuel Wiseman   Thomas Woollett*

# The Search Begins

In the summer of 1989 Wendell Kempton asked ABWE's astute treasurer, Bill Pierson, to begin investigating different areas for the possible relocation of the mission. The Search Committee looked at a total of 23 different properties, beginning in greater Harrisburg, Pennsylvania, which had a new airport and an outstanding road system.

A friend of the mission, Gary Helsel, had discussed the benefits of the Harrisburg area with Bill Pierson and Wendell Kempton, and, on October 10, Bill drove to Harrisburg to meet Gary and his real estate broker friend Bob Hughes. Bill spent two days with these men gathering information about the cost of property, cost of living, and the rates of local and state taxes. Bill found the cost of living to be lower than in Cherry Hill. He brought this information back to headquarters, and shared it with the president and PAC.

In light of the fact that living in the Harrisburg area would be less expensive than Cherry Hill, and that there would be several staff retirements in the near future, the Search Committee presented their findings to the ABWE board on July 13, 1990, for consideration and prayer. At the same meeting, the board asked the committee to conduct a similar study of other areas, which eventually included properties in Indiana, Ohio, Michigan, and Missouri. After considering all those areas it was clear to the committee that Harrisburg was as economical, if not more so, than any of the others evaluated.

On the evening of October 21 the Search Committee returned to Harrisburg to take another look. They met with realtor Bob Hughes; Jim Grandon, president of Jack Gaughen Realtors; land architect Ed Black; and Cass Santos, recently retired pastor from Bible Baptist Church of Shiremanstown, Pennsylvania. The following day the two men from Jack Gaughen Realtors rented a bus, showing the Search Committee approximately 18 properties in the greater Harrisburg area. One of them was the Capitol View Estates owned by Michael McKinney. The nearly 9,500-square-foot home overlooked the Susquehanna Valley, the city of Harrisburg, and the Blue Mountains north of town.

Bill Pierson would later recall, "The day we took this trip was absolutely some of the worst weather I have seen. It poured rain all day long, and the bus leaked. After a short time we could see water running down the aisle of the bus! That blustery day we saw the buildings, but because of low visibility we never did see the splendor of the property until a later date."

In a brief report to the Cherry Hill staff Bill stated, "This survey is very preliminary. We will keep you posted. Please pray that God will give us special leading to know His perfect will as it relates to staying where we are or relocating."

Two weeks later, Mr. and Mrs. Robert Austin, Rev. and Mrs. Gerald Montgomery, and the Piersons returned to Harrisburg to look again at the four properties that had been narrowed down as possible sites for the relocation of ABWE. These included two farms on the east shore of the Susquehanna River, near the Pennsylvania Turnpike on the road leading to the Harrisburg airport. A third site was vacant land on the river's west shore in an area known as Beacon Hill.

The fourth possibility was the McKinney property. On this visit they were able to see the impressive view, the spacious land area, and were able to tour the mansion.

After narrowing the four possibilities down to the Beacon Hill and McKinney properties, the committee asked for help from a land development expert. Earl Scarland, a good friend of Wendell Kempton's from Albany, New York, was invited to look at the two properties. His opinion was decisive: The McKinney property was better by far. With this additional support, the committee agreed to make Mike McKinney an offer.

At the annual ABWE meeting in April, the president boldly stated to the board that a third move of ABWE head-quarters was definitely possible. He said, "As we look at the future, we must be very sensitive to costs of operation. We are where we are today because of decisions we made 19 years ago. Good decisions must now be made so that the ABWE operation can continue 25 years from now. Our great ambi-tion is to serve our churches and their missionaries. Our goal is to expedite this service with excellence and with the least amount of future financial obligation. Costs will increase. Costs of operation will be higher, and the cost of living will climb. But we need to monitor a minimal financial demand from our churches, while further seeking to do well for our employees. We have tried to maintain a balanced position, a conservative but progressive philosophy.

"Will this mean a new location? I believe it will, but there are several important matters we must keep in mind:

- We must be led of God, and we need prayer.
- The board is unanimous in their support of searching out this matter.
- We will seek to keep everyone updated.
- We will not move unless we can sell our present property.

- We will not go into debt.
- There will be board involvement in all areas of this process.
- A move will probably take us to what would be considered an interior city.
- We will do all we can to keep our present team together.
- Financial assistance will have to be considered for the staff if we move.
- Usually, a move of this magnitude stirs up various kinds of emotional response.
- We assure everyone that we are only interested in doing God's perfect will."

From the outset, the mission leadership's sincere desire was to know the unfolding will of God. Board members unanimously agreed to the principle of building a new facility debt-free and without taking missionary support money from the churches. Above all, the entire team was determined to move along with an harmonious spirit.

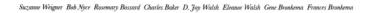

*Suzanne Weigner  Bob Nyce  Rosemary Bossard  Charles Baker  D. Jay Walsh  Eleanor Walsh  Gene Bronkema  Frances Bronkema*

1. Wendell W. Kempton, president of ABWE.
2. Project engineer Ralph Gruenberg and his wife Evelyn.

# An Unforgettable Coffee Break

Ralph Gruenberg, senior pastor of North Baptist Church in Rochester, New York, had an active bilingual (English and Spanish) urban ministry. The work was going well and evidencing God's blessing, but he and his wife, Evelyn, were beginning to realize their energy at this stage of life was only marginally adequate for the demanding work. They made their concern a matter for prayer.

For the moment, other things demanded their attention. It was time to load their red 1980 Dodge and head for the April ABWE board meetings in Cherry Hill. Ralph was a member of the Advisory Council and counted the 700-mile round trip a part of his commitment to the Great Commission.

During a coffee break at those meetings, Wendell Kempton drew Ralph aside and said, "Ralph, you have been on my mind lately. We're thinking seriously of moving ABWE from Cherry Hill to a new location near Harrisburg, if property becomes available. I've been thinking that you should head up the design and building of this project. Wouldn't this be a good time for you to retire from the pastorate and join ABWE for this and future projects?"

Surprised but honored by the proposal, Ralph later

whispered to Evelyn, "Honey, you won't believe what Wendell just dumped on me. He suggested that we consider joining ABWE full time to head up a new building project." Stunned, she exclaimed, "I can't believe this!" As the meeting was called to order, both Gruenbergs wondered if this proposal was God's providence.

After making his proposal to Ralph, Wendell admonished, "Take your time and pray. We both must be certain of God's leading. I'll be in touch with you soon."

Wendell hadn't asked just any mature pastor to consider such a major assignment. He knew from past association that Ralph held a civil engineering degree and current licenses. Ralph graduated from the New Jersey Institute of Technology in 1951, the same year he married Evelyn. For the next 12 years he was employed as a civil engineer.

As a young Christian, Ralph had been greatly influenced toward missionary service at the Madison Avenue Baptist Church of Patterson, New Jersey, under the ministry of Pastor Richard Seume. However, as Ralph puts it, "I was wide open to missions, but felt at that time it was God's will for me to continue my civil engineering training."

Ralph worked his way through college in a local municipal consulting firm. In 1950, a year before graduation, he took a summer job with the U.S. Bureau of Reclamation on the Columbia Basin Irrigation Project in eastern Washington state. At that time, the Columbia Basin was the biggest irrigation project in the world, getting its water from the Grand Coulee Dam, the world's largest dam. The project involved developing more than a million acres of desolate sagebrush into highly productive farmland to attract thousands of pioneers from all over the West.

While working on the Columbia Basin project, the Gruenbergs teamed up with other believers to start the First Baptist Church of Othello, Washington. In 1954, Ralph accepted a new job in Kansas City, Kansas. The Gruenbergs joined the living room nucleus that became Oak Grove Baptist Church, pastored by Rev. James Gray. While there, Ralph began to sense God's call to enter the ministry. Pastor Gray and his close-knit congregation strongly encouraged Ralph in his decision.

From 1957 to 1961 Ralph studied part time at Baptist Bible Seminary in Johnson City, New York, while working full time leading heavy construction projects throughout the Northeast. He and the seminary's athletic coach, Wendell Kempton, were both active members in the First Baptist Church of Johnson City. It was there that the friendship between the two men started.

Full-time Christian ministry began in 1962 when Ralph joined the staff of First Baptist as director of Christian education. Three years later, on Easter Sunday, he answered a call to become pastor of First Baptist Church in Belmont, New York.

Over a period of 27 years the Gruenbergs pastored four churches. In each of them Ralph led the congregation in major building or rebuilding projects. Most of those pastoral years were spent in Rochester, New York, where they now faced another major life-changing decision.

As he had promised during the April board meetings, Wendell Kempton kept in touch with Ralph by phone. Two months after the coffee break challenge, Ralph and Evelyn determined it was God's will for them to join ABWE. Though it was difficult to inform their church, they did so convinced of God's call to new horizons. Wendell Kempton now had a project engineer even though the building site had yet to be selected.

1. Capitol View Manor, as seen from Lewisberry Road.  2. One of the smaller buildings attached to the property.  3. Inner courtyard of the main house.

*Bill Wemett  Jan Wemett  Jim Garnham  Jon Delavan  Ty Whitney  Calvin Self  Margaret Self  Bob Chitwood  Max Pfoutz  Gordon Cummings*

# Capturing the Prize

On April 10, just prior to ABWE's annual board meeting, the Search Committee met again to review the options of staying in Cherry Hill, moving to another part of the country, or moving to Harrisburg. In the end, God's Spirit led them to revisit the McKinney property near Harrisburg, just outside the village of New Cumberland.

Mike McKinney's property was listed for $2.8 million, a reasonable price considering that it contained 134.19 acres of fields and woods, wrapped around a hill with a panoramic view of the Susquehanna Valley and the city of Harrisburg. The property included the beautiful mansion home of Mike McKinney, a small apartment building, a five-bedroom ranch home, a 10,000-sq.-ft. storage barn, a small horse barn, nearly two miles (9,000 L.F.) of board fencing, and a fish pond. An added benefit to the property was its location, one mile from the intersection of I-76 (Pennsylvania Turnpike) and I-83.

However, there was one major problem: The beautiful property the Search Committee had located was priced far higher than the mission could afford. Initial efforts at making lower offers through real estate agent Bob Hughes proved unsuccessful. Mike McKinney knew the value of his property and didn't want to budge in the stipulated selling price. After two visits with the owner, Bill Pierson approached Wendell Kempton and said, "The Finance Committee wants you to go and negotiate the price." Obtaining Bob Hughes' blessing, Wendell set up an appointment.

Driving up to Capitol View Manor that day, Wendell was filled with apprehension and wonderment. He faced a big assignment and nothing short of divine intervention would change the owner's mind. He consoled himself, "If this is the property God wants for ABWE, He will help us get it." Breathing a prayer, he rang the doorbell.

Negotiations began with much lower offers, but Mike stuck to his asking price of $2.8 million. Wendell looked at him and said, "Mr. McKinney, I come as a servant of God on behalf of the mission's Finance Committee, and representing a mission organization of over 1,000 missionaries serving around the world. I am only able to offer you $1.8 million. It is our final offer. I cannot go any higher. It's all we can afford."

Mike kindly replied, "Wendell Kempton, that is $1 million lower than I would ever consider. Go again and look at the property. I have listed everything, and the prices of all I have invested." After a few silent moments Wendell heard Mike McKinney say something the owner never dreamed he would say, "For some reason, known only to God, I will accept your offer." Wendell would testify later, "I was with Mr. McKinney all by myself. But God was there, and He did the rest. That was a miracle!"

One of Wendell's most exciting and historic releases to the ABWE board occurred on May 10, 1991, one month after the annual meetings. "This is a brief communiqué to share with you that a special board meeting is being called for Thursday, May 23, 1991, at 1:00 p.m. The meeting will be held in Harrisburg, Pennsylvania. Our purpose is to show you the property which has been under consideration for the past nine months. The Finance Committee has reached a decision with the owner. We are ready to submit a recommendation to you for your action.

"This property is considered a choice location. We ask you to sincerely call upon God for this urgent meeting. We have an agreement between owner and buyer contingent upon board and township approval. If we move ahead with these two prerequisites, then all the ABWE staff will have an opportunity to view the property at a later date. After visiting the site, we will enter into a time of prayer and discussion, followed by a vote. Please pray for God's perfect will."

Rev. Richard Christen, Rev. Will Davis, Rev. Robert Dyer, Jr., Dr. Carl Elgena, Dr. Kenneth Elgena, Rev. Lawrence Fetzer, Dr. Daniel Gelatt, Dr. Ollie Goad, Dr. Jack Jacobs, Rev. Earl Leiby, Rev. Gerald Montgomery, Mr. Robert Austin, Mr. William Parmerlee, Mr. Robert Reese, Dr. Mark Jackson, Mr. William Pierson, Dr. Wendell Kempton, and advisory council member, Rev. Ralph Gruenberg, attended that historic meeting of May 23, 1991.

The meeting in Harrisburg's Marriott Hotel began promptly at 1:00 p.m. and centered around the McKinney property. After spending several hours touring the site, the group spent two more hours in prayer and discussion. The strategic location of the property was emphasized: 1¾ hours to Philadelphia; ¾ of an hour to Baltimore; 2 hours to Washington, DC; 3¾ hours to New York City; 3¾ hours to Pittsburgh; and 2¼ hours to Scranton. It was also noted that Harrisburg is a state capital and statistics substantiated that operations would be more economical in the Harrisburg area than in Cherry Hill.

After a thorough evaluation of the pros and cons, Gerald Montgomery made the motion, seconded by Jack Jacobs, to purchase 134.19 acres in Fairview Township known as the McKinney property for $1.8 million, with the understanding that the purchase was contingent on township approval, environmental Phase I study, wetland review, and state approval for access to Route 114, known as Lewisberry Road.

Because of the importance of the decision, Wendell Kempton abandoned tradition and called for a written vote. After the group spent more time on their knees in prayer, Jerry Montgomery collected and counted the 19 ballots. He smiled and announced, "The vote is unanimous." The group began to sing spontaneously *Praise God From Whom All Blessings Flow*.

Wendell then proposed that the Gruenbergs move to the site as soon as possible after ABWE received Fairview Township supervisors' approval to proceed. He estimated that the decision should be official by November 1, 1991. Everyone at that historic meeting felt that they had been buoyed along by the Spirit of the Lord. At 9:50 p.m. Wendell closed the meeting in prayer.

In a special release to the churches and the ABWE family president Kempton said, "We are aware that this possible move will have a major impact upon the future of the mission. We are only interested in following God's perfect will. You should be aware that there was a great spirit among the board during our time together in Harrisburg. Thank you for your prayers as we continue to take these steps of faith in seeking God's perfect will."

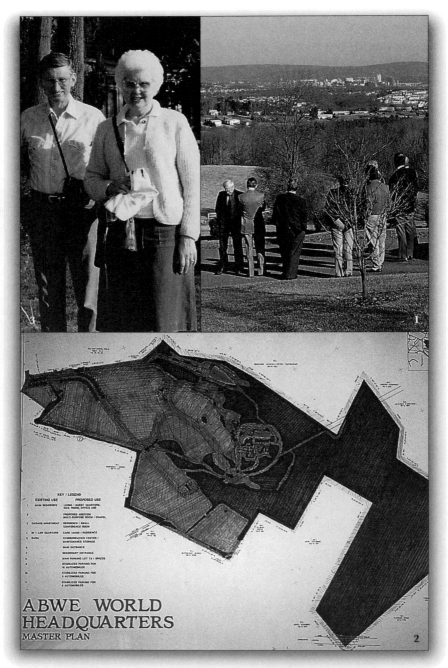

1. Building committee members on site.  2. Topographical plan of the new property.  3. Rev. and Mrs. Gerald Montgomery, board members and part of the search and building committees.

# Gearing Up for Action

**D**eciding to purchase the McKinney property set the stage for the formation of a building committee. The committee was composed of Chairman Bill Pierson, Donald Davis, Robert Dyer, Jr., Robert Austin, Gerald Montgomery, E. C. Haskell, Sandra Lyons, and Mary Ann Eckman. Wendell Kempton, Ralph Gruenberg, Ruth Kempton, and Betty Pierson served as ex-officio members. Permission to start building now rested with the Fairview Township supervisors and Zoning Board.

Their first meeting with the township supervisors introduced ABWE to the community. On August 29, Wendell Kempton and attorney Jerry Duffie gave sworn testimony about the background of ABWE, its purpose, and what the mission intended to accomplish on the property. Wendell gave an overview of the proposed land development, told what would be done with roads, trees, septic systems, and wetlands. His goal was to assure township authorities that there would be no adverse effect if the mission developed the land. He also pointed out that extensive contacts had already been made with many of the local residents to give them a clear understanding of ABWE's identity and plans. Before a final vote could be taken, however, the Zoning Board wanted clarification of the traffic study, evidence of an application for wetlands approval, and a letter from PennDOT (Pennsylvania Department of Transportation) granting direct access to Lewisberry Road.

On September 26, in a final meeting with township officials, Wendell Kempton, Bill Pierson, and ABWE's corporate counsel Don Davis, along with local attorney Jerry Duffie, went before the Zoning Board again. At that meeting the supervisors approved ABWE's plan, pending PennDOT's approval to access Lewisberry Road. A 1.91 acre plot of roadside land would have to be purchased from Mr. & Mrs. Roderick Mills to make that access possible.

Wendell later wrote about that meeting, "Praise be to God! I am happy to report that the Fairview Township Zoning Board voted unanimously to approve our petition to use the McKinney property as our future mission headquarters. The zoning commissioners commended us on our presentation. Their decision will be ratified in writing in November followed by a 30-day appeal period wherein township residents will have an opportunity to request that the Zoning Board decision be overturned. This is unlikely since there hasn't been opposition by the residents from the very beginning."

An amazing sidelight is what traffic engineers discovered during the studies required for the PennDOT access permit. On that entire section of Lewisberry Road only one 75-foot stretch met the criteria for permitted access. That parcel was available for purchase, and almost exactly where ABWE wanted to connect. Does providence extend to how a state road was constructed years ago?

In November, after all the official obstacles had been overcome, ABWE's Board of Trustees approved the purchase of two properties: the 134.19 acre tract in Fairview Township, York County, for $1.8 million, and the 1.91 acres from Mr. and

Mrs. Roderick Mills for $70,000. As the year ended, in a memo entitled *A Time For Rejoicing*, President Wendell Kempton announced, "Today we closed on the proposed properties. Mr. Pierson represented the mission. The papers have now been officially signed and we are the owners. GREAT THINGS HE HATH DONE!"

There can be no doubt that the gracious hand of God superintended the events between the time of the board's first exposure to the property on May 23, 1991, and the sale closure on December 3, 1991. God's perfect will had been accomplished.

1. Rev. Joseph Stowell, senior board member, wields the shovel. 2. Staff and friends at ground-breaking ceremony. 3. Bob Hughes points out view to Bill Pierson. 4. The project officially begins.

*Gladys Geshay  Don Beckett  Ray Dunn  Ted Walborn  Harmon Bergen  John Geshay  Jack Daam  Wayne Sickler  Don Grollimund*

# The Golden Shovel

As soon as the new property purchase was finalized, President Kempton shifted into high gear. He composed the following letter early in January 1992 and sent it to 8,000 pastors:

"This is an unusual letter for me to write. I trust you will take a moment to read it. It is of great significance to the advance of the gospel worldwide. In the past few years several mission agencies have had to move from the New Jersey area, including the following: Trans World Radio, Christian and Missionary Alliance, Sudan Interior Mission, International Bible Society, International Missions, Pocket Testament League, and AMG International. All of them moved because this area has become very expensive.

"ABWE has also been confronted with the same economic challenges. How can we best serve our local churches and their missionaries in the most frugal manner? How can we continue concentrating our resources for missionary support and evangelism? As we look into the future, we cannot justify a continued presence in this rather prestigious area. When we moved here 21 years ago it was a middle class area. Today it is upper middle class and upper class.

"Our mission has now made the decision to relocate

near Harrisburg, Pennsylvania. This removes us from the high-cost corridor while keeping us close to our roots. It places us in an interior city with a great arterial system and a good airport. Harrisburg is in a country setting and is far more moderate in its cost of housing, taxes, car insurance, and utilities. I anticipate the move to take place in July–August 1993. We would ask you to pray with us regarding the following:

- The sale of our present property in Cherry Hill.
- The necessary funds to build on the new property.
- Wisdom to make the right decisions.
- The miracle of moving there debt free for the glory of God.

"This is a giant undertaking and a big step of faith, but we believe that it will afford all of us the opportunity to see God at work during a time in which we must trust Him with all of our hearts.

"You will receive a letter within the next ten days that will offer your people an exciting opportunity to be directly involved in this project. Project engineer Ralph Gruenberg will endeavor to build our new headquarters for God's glory with volunteer craftsmen.

"It is a high honor to team up with you for the cause of world evangelism. I want to thank you and your church for all that you have done for our ABWE missionaries as well as for others. Great things He hath done!"

In his January release to the ABWE board, Wendell wrote, "Please pray that God will raise up a minimum of 200 volunteer craftsmen who will be used to build the international headquarters. If you know of men and women who would be willing to give a week of their time, please contact Ralph Gruenberg. He comes to us with broad experience in building projects at home and abroad, and with 30 years of pastoral experience."

Ralph and Evelyn moved to the building site in early February 1992, taking up residence in the hilltop manor. Ralph immediately began to work on site plans and building plans with Roger Petrone, a Christian architect who volunteered his services. Ralph also worked on numerous legal matters that needed to be addressed and approved before a building permit would be issued. These legal matters included environmental impact statements, surface water management plans, drainage protection of the wetlands, hazardous waste studies, water supply approvals, soil percolation tests, sanitary waste disposal, and negotiations with a gas company whose underground pipes ran very close to the construction area. To speed the process, the emerging building plans were given regular informal reviews by state and township officials. Architect Roger Petrone not only had a design challenge, he also had a tricky logistical challenge with constant time pressure.

In the meantime, Wendell Kempton notified the ABWE board that their annual meeting would be held at the Ramada Inn at the junction of the Pennsylvania Turnpike (I-76) and I-83, in New Cumberland. The meeting would include a tour of the new property. The board members were advised to "dress casually and wear comfortable walking shoes (rain gear might also be a good idea, just in case)."

On April 14 the board and staff members met for a time of prayer. Ralph explained the blueprints of the property and told what he intended to accomplish, the methods he planned to use, and his hope to achieve the goals with maximum stewardship.

Wendell outlined a series of target dates. "Lord willing, construction will begin on August 15. We hope to have the building under roof by Christmas. The target date for completing the project is July 4, 1993. We anticipate being moved in and fully operational by Labor Day. This will involve a

Ed Fortner  David Jones  Larry Bach  William Cole  Debra Daam  Earl Riegsecker  Donna Riegsecker  Daniel Riegsecker  William Parmerlee

major investment in the lives of many believers who have a heart for missions. Many are giving up vacation time and will pay their own expenses to be a part of this endeavor."

Everyone on the construction team recognized that starting such a large building complex in the fall could involve serious weather risks. But they also felt pressure to move ahead during months that volunteer availability might be highest.

After the Ramada Inn meeting, the board and staff drove to the site for the groundbreaking ceremony. Members of the Search and Finance committees were present, along with the architect, Roger Petrone. Special guests Gary Helsel, project clerk, and Bob Hughes, real estate agent, were also present. Dr. Joseph Stowell, Sr., wielded the golden shovel. As he turned the first shovelful of earth he smiled and said, "I've done the easy part." All joined in singing *Great Is Thy Faithfulness*. Dr. Stowell, ABWE's senior board member, having served for over 50 years, led in a prayer of dedication. A local TV crew videotaped the ceremony, which was shown on the six o'clock news.

*David Parmerlee  Roy Garthwaite  Timothy M. Smith  Tom Bolles  George Monsell  Chad Felmlee  Ken Rice  Davis Deiner  James Humphreys*

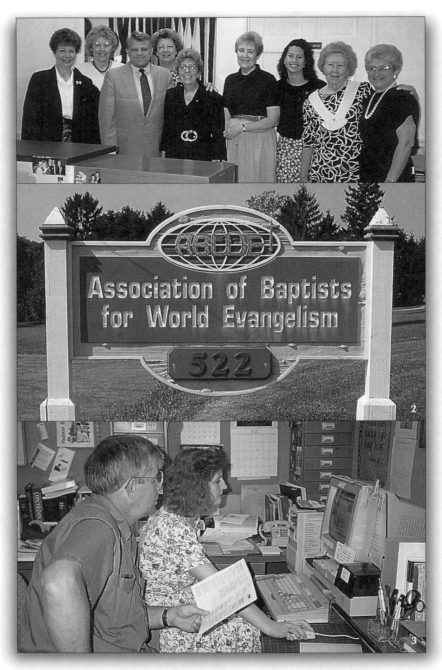

1. Cherry Hill staff: some moved, some stayed.   2. The staff also volunteered to help construct the new headquarters.   3. Staff members were asked to work right up to moving day.

*Allen Kashner  Donald Wetzel  William Zimmerman  Doug Nichols  Josh Sorber  Nancy Shillingford  Connee Keefe  Paul Sears  Stephen Bruni*

# Preparing the Staff

From the outset of this gigantic undertaking, Wendell Kempton carried a special burden for the Cherry Hill staff. He eloquently addressed this matter in a poignant communication titled "Our Philosophy of Relocation."

***Our utmost desire is to encourage the planning and building committee.***

These people will be involved in investing extra time in behalf of this project. They will also be in a position where they must think creatively and objectively. Many of their decisions will affect the design, layout, and overall function of the building. The importance of this committee comes into focus when one understands that we will have to minister more effectively within this new environment. They will also be aware that their decisions will be of long tenure, affecting and influencing all who follow us in this ministry. Sensing this awesome assignment, they will need cheerleaders from time to time.

***Our utmost desire is to involve you in this process.***

We will allow everyone to share his or her ideas, concepts, desires, and concerns. The committee will meet with the various divisions within the mission and individuals to solicit input. We are zealous to have everyone involved. Each individual is important to the success of this project. This is a rare opportunity that seldom comes into our lives. May we, together, have an uninhibited, creative, common sense, inspired team effort.

### *Our utmost desire is to strive to be good stewards.*

This stewardship will involve our time, our investment, our space allocation, and our costs for the total project. These next 21 months will fly by. Every week will be very important. How we use time will be crucial. All the days must be counted as well as the planning of minor and major events, the sequence of those happenings, and the flow. Each day is a link that ties into another. They all have to be in order, and they will finally end up being that inseparable chain. Perhaps this is something of what the wise man was saying when he wrote: "Prepare your outside work. Make it fit for yourself in the field, and afterwards build your house" (Proverbs 24:27).

The proper use of space is also of great importance. Since we may be more aware of this science now than when we built in Cherry Hill, we will give this our careful attention. The design and layout of the building is key. It will be wise for the committee to sit with several consultants. This should not hinder or curb individuals, departments, or the committee in their aspirations or even dreams. We must be free to think big, think small, think wisely, and think objectively. Our goal is to end up with a facility that is more functional. It must result in a design and layout that seek to maximize every inch of space. This may mean a smaller building. It may mean a larger one. Smaller space does not necessarily mean restriction and confinement. Larger space does not guarantee proper use of space or even expansion. The rooms can only be divided and subdivided in so many ways. Everyone will be confronted with big decisions. It is for this reason that the decisions must be good ones, ones that can be justified and lined up with previous decisions and those that will follow.

Raymond Gould, Jr.  John E. Johnson  Richard Mastin  Paul Spotts  Chuck Boscaljan  Tom Fuhr  Chris Marks  Leslie Parsons  John Parsons

There is also stewardship of dollars. At this writing there are only estimates as to what will be the total cost of this project. We will monitor and be careful to watch every expenditure. This will take time as comparisons will be made prior to purchases of all material. We will strive to build with the very best material and for the best price. Our goal will be to do things right.

Presently, commercial builders tell us that we can build in the Harrisburg area for $65.00 per square foot. There will be other substantial expenditures such as the construction of a road into the property. Unexpected costs are always part of any project. This all adds up to big dollars. I am sure that God has given us the kind of leadership that will ensure the board, staff, missionary family, and donors of a job well done, and all within the framework of a budget.

***Our utmost desire is to build much of the new building with volunteer help.***

Most people tell us that this cannot be done during this hour of history. My response is, "You may be right, but we are going to do it." We desire to use craftsmen who will volunteer a week of their vacation time assisting us with the project. We will have to carefully plan each event so that the specified laborers are present. Churches will have to be enlisted. Pastors will have to promote this among their people. Churches and pastors will make a commitment to this project and principle. From their congregations they will send gifted and willing servants. If the Amish can raise up a house or barn and if the Jehovah's Witnesses can build their headquarters building with volunteer labor, then our churches can also enter into such with all their hearts. We, too, are committed to the principle of volunteerism. This is how the bulk of the labor will be done.

*Silas Newman   Mel Lacock   Carol McCaffery   Charles Newell   Jim Dunn   Donald Hankin   Mark Halko   Vicky Madeira   Dolores Franz*

*Our utmost desire is to move through every step
with a prayerful spirit.*

We will need much more than we have, much more
than we are, and much more than any consultant can share.
Our best position in the future will be that of a child. At our
best we know very little, have little to offer, and are incapable
of the task before us. Even if we have gathered experience in
our past, we dare not lean too heavily upon it. We must always
pray. This will take time, but God honors those who are as little children. Honest humility is one of the greatest qualities we
can take as we pursue our goals. No one in world history has
ever traveled down this road before. God has set this one out
for us. We cannot improve upon: "Trust in the Lord with all
thine heart; and lean not unto thine own understanding. In all
thy ways acknowledge Him, and He shall direct thy paths"
(Proverbs 3:5,6).

Prayer must preface, prevail, and follow every aspect of
our venture of faith. It is prayer that will give us discernment
and wisdom. It will be prayer that will keep us quiet, content,
and full of faith. Prayer will strengthen those who are left
behind. Prayer will sell our homes and sell our present property. It will guide us in the timing of all these important events.
Intercession will help all of us with our patience and perseverance. Prayer will help us stay together (though some will
depart), support one another, assist us as we move through
transition, find other good jobs, and enable us to give thanks
in all things. It will help us to be like Christ. Prayer will make
this new road a bright and shining path in our life and mission
experience.

All of this is rather scary. None of us has taken enough
courses on properly handling the unknown. For most of us the
unknown confronts us with darkness. It sensitizes our emotions and captures our imaginations. We wonder how will it
all work out. We think it is coming at the wrong time of our

lives. I sure hope Kempton knows what he is doing. Charting unknown waters can strike fear into our minds and hearts. It can make us reluctant to enter the boat for the journey. It is great to be intimately acquainted with the One who calms storms and walks on water. He will be walking along our side and even be in our boat. The Shepherd is experienced in leading His sheep to other fields, as well as taking us through uncharted waters. *Lead On, O King Eternal.* May You be honored and glorified through it all.

PLEASE INDICATE YOUR MAIN SKILLS AND PREFERENCES BY A "1." MARK OTHER THINGS YOU
ARE ABLE/WILLING TO DO WITH A "2."

[ 2 ] General Construction
        Labor/Helper

[   ] Working on the FOOD SERVICE
        for the gang.

[ 2 ] Clearing Timber and Brush.

[ 2 ] Concrete work. Check what
        you do.

    ___ form work

    ✓ setting re-bars and mesh

    ✓ placing

    ✓ finishing

    ___ sidewalks and steps

[ / ] Masonry

    ✓ block

    ✓ brick

    ✓ stone

    ___ ceramic tile

[   ] Steel Work

[ / ] Carpentry

    ✓ rough

    ✓ finishing/trim

    ✓ roof trusses

    ✓ windows and doors

    ___ counters, cabinets, etc.

[ 2 ] Roofing

    ✓ shingles

    ✓ other

[   ] Electrical

[   ] Heating, Ventilating,
        Air conditioning

[   ] Walls and Ceilings

    ___ plaster

    ___ drywall

    ___ suspended ceilings

[   ] Plumbing

[   ] Telephone System Installation

[   ] Computer System Installation

[   ] Shortwave Radio Installation

[   ] Security System Installation

[   ] Painting, wood finishing

[   ] Wallpapering

[   ] Carpet laying

[ ✓ ] Floor tile

[   ] Landscaping

[   ] Cleanup

[ ✓ ] Moving in help

**1**

1. Sample form that Ralph Gruenberg sent to volunteers.
2. Project engineer Ralph Gruenberg in his field office.  3. Jerry Duffie.

# Off and Running

Like a shot from a starter's gun, the ABWE team was off and running. In Cherry Hill the staff began to take seriously the prospects of uprooting: selling their homes, purchasing new ones, moving and adjusting to a new life in a new location. In Harrisburg, Ralph and Evelyn began to take their gigantic challenge in stride. Even before their arrival, Ralph initiated the volunteer recruiting process. Now, in his thorough way, he began sending periodic volunteer newsletters to the churches.

As Wendell Kempton had promised, Ralph sent the following letter, including response forms, to pastors around the country and to the ABWE missionary family:

"I am looking for some good people. Not famous preachers or spectacular musicians. Not writers, or even missionaries. I'm looking for grass-roots people who could be involved for a week or two (or some other time span) in a unique project.

"The Amish flock together to help build a house or barn. The Seventh-Day Adventists and Mennonites have their projects. So do the Mormons. Why can't Bible-believing, missions-minded Baptists do the same to build a new mission headquarters?

"By now you may have heard that ABWE is moving to Harrisburg to escape pricey Cherry Hill. It's an effort toward better stewardship of the mission's dollar. We want to further stretch some specially donated funds by building as much as possible with volunteer help. I will begin the design and construction, starting February 6, 1992.

"Take a look at the enclosed form. Do you have anyone with the interest and skills listed? Why not challenge them to involvement in this missions effort? I believe this opportunity can be a great experience of ministry and fellowship. Have people send their forms to me soon. Encourage them to contact me with questions. Assure them that this will be a carefully coordinated effort where we will maximize everyone's efforts and skills.

"I estimate construction will begin August 15, 1992. July 2, 1993, is our completion target. We hope to have the office move completed by September 1, 1993. From about September 15 to December 1, 1992, will be the big push to get the building closed in before the harsh winter sets in. I'll really need some good-size crews to get off to a quick start. Of course, that's only the beginning. I'll need all kinds of skills for the various stages of the work. I hope you will help me in creating interest. Pastors like you are the key to seeing this happen for God's glory. If you need more forms, call or write me. THANKS!"

While that letter was circulating, Ralph was already starting the complex permit process with township, county, and state officials. He asked for prayer for this and for the need of immediate volunteers to do pre-construction grounds preparation, which required a special concession from the Fairview Township supervisors. Jerry Duffie, ABWE's attorney, worked for a firm that represented Fairview Township, so Jerry could not represent the mission in matters pertaining to the township. He recommended Ron Lucas, a specialist in land-use planning and zoning matters, who negotiated ABWE's zoning with Fairview Township. Ralph was still on target to begin the earth-moving work on July 1, and hoped the building permit would be issued by August 15. Every day was critical with winter coming on.

Regarding the Cherry Hill property, Wendell Kempton reported to the board, "There is still no movement as it relates to a potential buyer. Several groups have recently gone through the building to look it over. I know you are keenly interested and are praying. We urge you to continue to knock on the door of heaven regarding this important matter."

1. Jay Walsh, project host.  2. Stan and Jean Holman, retired missionaries, who were unable to serve on site due to ill health.  3. Eleanor Walsh, project hostess.

*Jeannette Sunday  Mary Ann Meals  Dorothy Minium  Debbie Siwils  Maye Lundeen  Vicki Santos  Janet Fair  Joy Linebaugh  Kame Reed*

# Chaplain and Hostess

Ralph's poignant appeal for volunteers, also sent to all ABWE missionaries, arrived in Jay and Eleanor Walsh's mailbox in Chittagong, Bangladesh. In light of their upcoming June 1992 furlough, and willing to spend a week or two helping on the project, Jay filled out the volunteer form. He had no special building skills to offer (although he had supervised the construction of many mission building projects in Bangladesh), but indicated his willingness to wield a hammer, mix cement, or do anything that would be of help. He also volunteered Eleanor's services as a cook without consulting her. When she read over the form she firmly said, "Don't volunteer me as a cook! I am willing to help in the kitchen, but I am not a cook." After suitably amending the form, Jay mailed it to Ralph on May 29, 1992.

The Walshes arrived in Grand Rapids, Michigan, on June 20 and spent the next several weeks settling their home. They were eagerly anticipating the Missionary Enrichment Conference in Clark's Summit, Pennsylvania, and visiting ABWE's new property near Harrisburg.

July 9 proved to be an auspicious day for the Walshes. Their car muffler had to be replaced, an electrician repaired the lighting fixtures in their basement, and that afternoon they received an unexpected phone call from Ralph Gruenberg. He asked, "Would you folks consider working full time on the project as chaplain and hostess in place of Stan and Jean Holman? Stan is seriously ill, and they won't be able to fill those positions."

Stan and Jean Holman had served with ABWE in the Philippines for 39 years, so the Walshes knew them well. During those years Stan had carried the responsibility for almost every ABWE building project in the Philippines. He knew how to get things done. They were an ideal couple for the Harrisburg project. But God had different plans.

Two days after Ralph's call, Jay phoned the Holmans to get an update on Stan's situation. He had suffered a major stroke that left the right side of his body paralyzed. As he put it, "The Lord suddenly changed my direction. His ways are past finding out." Stan confirmed to Jay that he and Jean would be unable to move to Harrisburg as planned. That news meant that Jay and Eleanor had to seriously consider Ralph's proposal. They prayed that God's will would become clear when they met with the ABWE officials in July.

The Walshes arrived in Clark's Summit on July 17, their 38th wedding anniversary. That evening they met with Russ and Nancy Ebersole to discuss extending their furlough to cover for the Holmans. Russ, ABWE's administrator for the Far East, agreed. On the following day the Walshes met with President Kempton who strongly urged them to accept the new responsibilities. Bill and Betty Pierson also encouraged Jay and Eleanor in this special ministry, suggesting that they visit the building site.

On July 20 the Walshes drove to Harrisburg to meet the Gruenbergs. They also met two volunteers who would play a major role in the "miracle on the hill": David Greening, the first construction superintendent, and Sharon Hammaker, the gracious lady who planned meals for the volunteers until the Walshes arrived. That evening Jay and Eleanor enjoyed dinner with Ralph and Evelyn. After discussion regarding their future work responsibilities, Jay and Eleanor were persuaded that this was the job God had for them. They left the next day for Cherry Hill, promising to be on duty by the first of September.

The side trip to Cherry Hill to meet with Bill Pierson was motivated by a special request. Would the mission be agreeable to the Walshes living in the mansion on the mountain while construction was in process? That would make them the only residents living on the property. The Gruenbergs had wisely decided to live some distance away from the construction site, a place that would consume their time and energy for the following year. The Walshes' proposal was discussed and welcomed. They left for Grand Rapids with the confidence that they were following the will of their heavenly Father, and that everything was in place for a special year of ministry on the mountain.

Jay and Eleanor sought permission from their field council in Bangladesh and informed their supporting churches of their plans. After completing a speaking schedule and closing their home, the Walshes loaded necessary possessions in Gene and Fran Bronkema's pickup and trailer, and headed for Pennsylvania on August 31, 1992. The following morning the Walshes moved into the mansion on the hill, into the rooms now called the Executive Guest Suites #1 and #2. Those two rooms would be their home for the next 12 months.

1. The all-important building permit. 2. Earth-moving crew. 3. Laying block for the rotunda.

# Under Construction

In the spring of 1992 Ralph predicted that construction of the new half-mile access road to the property and the foundations of the building would start in August. His June report said, "Around here everything right now is moving at full speed: architectural detail plans, electrical design, HVAC (heating, ventilation, air conditioning), and plumbing designs. Temporary utility service agreements have been made.

"I'm continually hearing from more volunteers, establishing commercial credit with local suppliers, pausing once in awhile to admire the spectacular view, and shaking my head in ongoing wonder over the property God gave to ABWE and how He did it. We have entertained many visitors, volunteer prospects who, out of curiosity, dropped by to see the site."

Wendell Kempton informed the board, "God in His faithfulness has brought us to around the $1 million mark with commitments and cash. It is our great burden to accomplish the project without indebtedness and in a way that would not injure our missionary support or their projects. Two parties are interested in the Cherry Hill property. One has submitted an offer and the other is in the process. Some of our staff have already put their homes on the market. We have invited people of expertise from the Harrisburg area to orient our people as it pertains to banking and real estate. There is a good spirit here and our personnel are excited."

In his July *Volunteer Information Bulletin* Ralph thought aloud: "I've just been thinking. One year from now, Lord willing, our project will be completed. Humanly speaking, it's a bit scary because it all hangs on volunteers, not just enlisting, but reporting for duty. There is no contract. No performance bond. Just unusual commitment from hundreds of people. And trust. Confident that God will, through His people, demonstrate His power and faithfulness.

"From now on a fascinating story will continue to unfold. A story that involves hundreds of volunteers making a coordinated sacrifice of time and effort for the sake of world evangelism. They will follow through on a commitment that in most cases involves significant personal cost and inconvenience. Strange sounding words—almost foreign to our self-centered culture! But in missions they are everyday vocabulary. And missions is what we're involved in. Call it missions or call it ministry. It's part of the joy of serving the Lord, who saved us from the broad road that leads to certain and everlasting destruction. Actually, we ought to cancel the words *cost* and *inconvenience*. Let us on this project substitute the word *privilege*."

Ralph also wrote, "We've tried to get a head start where we could. A chain saw gang from Pastor Dan Gelatt's church (Washington Heights Baptist Church, Dayton, Ohio) has removed trees and brush. Local volunteers and ABWE staff have cleaned the barn, moved woodpiles, cleaned bathrooms (there are eight of them in the main house), transplanted 160 shrubs, removed wallpaper, mulched gardens, and done grounds cleanup. The first week in August will be Tom Sawyer week. We are expecting over 70 teens to paint the 9,000 feet of board fencing."

In August he reported, "A jillion trees have been cut.

Mountains of branches and brush are being reduced to chips and ashes. Our first silt trap is in place. The garage was demolished. I wish you could have observed the teens as they painted all the fencing! Heavy equipment is all around. Excavation is under way."

Ralph's goal was to have the official building permit in hand by the middle of August, but there were delays caused by unresolved differences of opinion on sewage disposal between the Department of Environmental Resources and the Fairview Township officials. Meanwhile, he received permission to construct forms for the footers, even though no concrete could be poured until the permit was in hand. The mission staff prayed earnestly for delivery of the all-important document.

One week later, it happened. Ralph jubilantly announced, "We had the foundation forms all in place and were anxiously waiting for that permit. At about 2:00 p.m. on August 24, nine more days closer to winter, it was delivered! Within an hour we were pouring our first concrete footers. That was when the work on the building began."

In thinking through what the year ahead of him would involve, Ralph decided he needed three qualified men to act as building superintendents, men who would be willing to serve up to four months apiece. David Greening from Muncy Valley, Pennsylvania, and Jerry VanHorne from Rochester, New York, were the first to volunteer. Ralph's prayer had been partially answered. Later, however, the Lord led David Purrington, a builder from Wheelersburg, Ohio, to volunteer for the final period. The team was in place!

Construction proceeded with a full head of steam. In October Wendell Kempton reported, "We are praising the Lord that approximately 75% of the road and parking lot is now finished. We are checking to see if the job can be finished with one layer of asphalt before winter sets in. The block work

1. Laying block for the basement. 2. Clearing the property for blacktopping.
3. Working on the Administration wing. 4. Architect Roger Petrone working on-site.
5. Exterior finish work on the rotunda. 6. The geothermal heat pump.

K. Kevin Pals  John Carlson  Rob Albright  Roy Brungard, Jr.  Barry Witzer  Michael Hall  Jeremy Hall  Chad Cole  John Esh  Chad Esh

1., 2. Raising walls for the new wings. 3. Matt Walsh, Randy Riegsecker, and Derek Purrington. 4. Roofing the building. 5. Dave Purrington (left) and Jerry VanHorne, construction supervisors.

*Evelyn Tworzydlo   Jack Tworzydlo   Dave Fleming   Daniel Ransom   Joan Fleming   Doug Nelson   Richard Overcash   Laban Wingert   Gary Gembe*

in the administrative wing has been completed. Framing and roof trusses are also in place. Cement block work for the rotunda, Corporate Finance, and Treasury wings is under way. An extensive amount of dynamiting had to be done. Dick Phelps and Fred Madeira are making available three large mobile homes for our staff who may need housing during the transition. We continue to be amazed at how God is supplying volunteers for the project. I am also praising the Lord for the $1.4 million in cash and commitments that have been promised and for a $500,000 matching gift. We have $100,000 of that, but still need the other $400,000!"

In a letter dated November 11, 1992, addressed to his ABWE colleagues in Cherry Hill, Ralph wrote: "This is my first report since joining the ABWE family last February. It has been an interesting nine months. From February to July the emphasis was on design and the obtaining of necessary permits and approvals for both the new headquarters building and the magnificent site where it will be located. Volunteer enlistment was also carried on during this time. Since then we have moved ahead with vigor. The building is going up!"

From mid-August until Christmas 1992 the "miracle on the mountain" was well on the way to becoming reality. Week after week the Lord sent wonderful groups of volunteers. There could be no question that the gracious hand of God was superintending the project that was moving along under the Heavenly Father's good favor.

When September ended, the new access road and parking lot had been completed. Trees had been removed from the construction areas, and the dynamiting crew had blown out the offending boulders. Foundation trenches for the first three phases of construction (administrative wing, corporate finance wing, and the rotunda) had been formed and poured. The floor and walls of the administration wing had been roughed in, ready for the roof rafters that had just been deliv-

*Harris Stuermer  Dale Barkulein  Jerome Redding  Don Phelps  Tom Kilpatrick  Sandy Rice  Drew Talbot  Joe Leather  Tom Betz  Larry Bixler*

ered. The rotunda basement floor had been poured and block work started.

On October 6 the huge thermogenic heating/cooling boiler was gently lifted off a flatbed truck and lowered into place on the rotunda floor, eventually to be enclosed in its special chamber. Later that month the retaining walls protecting the gasoline pipelines along the steep hillside were completed. The huge water tank that would serve the mission for years to come had been installed underground. Foundation work for the Missionary Finance and Media/Auditorium wings was under way. Both the Administration and Corporate Finance wings came under roof. It seemed like the volunteers were trying to prove they could build faster than architect Roger Petrone could furnish the plans. Roger always won, though sometimes only by hours!

November's chilling winds reminded us that winter was near. One morning work crews were amazed to discover that fierce winds the night before had stripped off the insulation sheathing, scattering it into the woods. By the end of the month the Missionary Finance wing was under roof and the most of the Media/Auditorium wing had been completed, made possible by a generous gift from one of the volunteers.

In December work crews were slim, but Ralph's goal to have the project completely under roof by Christmas had been accomplished. We celebrated our Savior's birth praising God for the great things He had done!

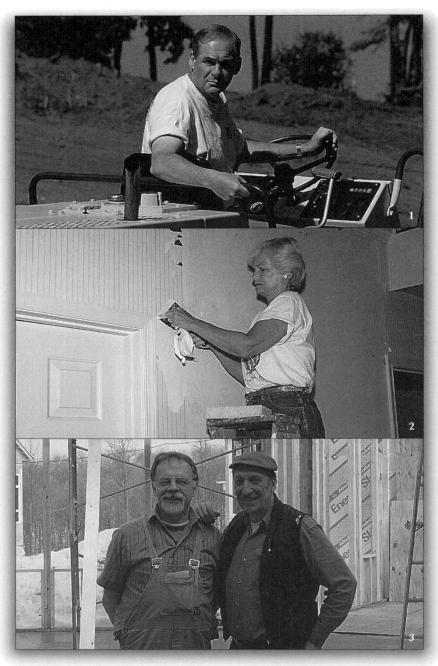

1. Wendell Kempton helped with earth moving.   2. Ruth Kempton painted and wall-papered.
3. Rev. Larry Armstrong (left), one of the ABWE missionaries who volunteered,
working with volunteer.

Ray LaBonte  Claudia Neiner  Jim Ranostay  Romyne Strickland  Ronald Faries  Doug Linebaugh  Bob Stimeare  Dave Palmer  Mario Pinto

# Proposals for the Trip

The first quarter of 1993 found the volunteers working with a roof over their heads. There were still great quantities of work to be accomplished. The annual meetings for April 12–13, 1993, were held at the Ramada Inn in New Cumberland. In his report under the title of "Proposals For The Trip," Dr. Kempton made several proposals: "These are not set in concrete," he said, "but they are serious proposals. I am trusting that these will be given serious consideration."

1) I propose that we begin in the near future to volunteer our time in the project at Harrisburg. I further suggest that it be organized in the following manner: There will be 12 trips, each made up of 10 of our personnel, men and women from all levels of the staff. I suggest that those involved leave Cherry Hill at 5:30 a.m. and depart from Harrisburg at 3:00 p.m. It will make a long day, but will allow you to be a part of this project. It will further signal to our missionaries and churches our sincere involvement. We would arrive on site at 7:45 a.m., begin work at 8:00 a.m. and labor for 6½ hours. All of us who have already been a part of this program have paid for our own meals.

David Allen  Terry Helwig  Joe Vance  Chris Cobb  Andy Smith  Ernest Winston  Michael Berry  Daniel Muller  Frank McQuade  David Harsh

2) I also suggest that the volunteer principle prevail throughout. I propose that those willing to be a part of the project
   do so without pay. Use one of your sick days or vacation
   days. In this way, you enter into the experience as a true
   volunteer. If we all participate, this will enable us to con-
   tribute 780 hours toward the volunteer program.

3) I propose that each individual move to Harrisburg at
   the best time for you. This means that some will move in
   March, while others will move in August or September.
   There will be a six- to seven-month moving timetable.
   If you move early, you will be expected to keep your
   responsibilities covered in Cherry Hill.

4) I propose that we move in the most economical manner.
   We are carefully considering bids submitted by professional movers. But, I am requesting that we consider
   moving ourselves. If it is planned properly, we could
   accomplish the task and save an estimated $50,000,
   renting U-Hauls. Perhaps we could hire high school
   or college students to help.

5) I am going to climb out on the limb even farther by
   proposing that all men who have one month of vacation
   consider reducing their vacation by 10 days in 1993.
   These 10 days would be used to move and get settled
   in the Harrisburg area.

Turning to finances, the president said, "Our goal is to
raise $1.8 million. God can and will provide in His way and
time. We all need to pray earnestly. I am aware that most of
you are involved in giving. I want to thank you for that. I am
sure you have given out of your hearts. Some of you have
given from savings. God has honored us in the past when we
as a staff have given extra, and He will do it again.

"We still have quite a way to go in order to meet our
goal. We are seeing a few thousand dollars come in each week;
some weeks as little as $3,000. Please pray that our goal will

be achieved. Remember that we seek to accomplish the goal in a way that does not injure our missionaries' support or projects."

Wendell also pointed out, "Even though we are all aware of our move and have had ample preparation, everyone will be psychologically touched. All of us will respond in different ways. Everyone will sense loss and may go through the pain of separation. To say good-bye to friends and relatives will demand inner strength and support. I am calling on our entire staff family to hold each other up in prayer before God. Quite a few of our people will be staying in New Jersey. Several will be moving after living here all their lives. Some would rather stay here but must move. All of us look upon the future with mixed emotions. There are so many uncertainties, but our biggest assignment will be sincerely entering into one another's experiences, whether it is staying or leaving.

"Let me share a few thoughts which I believe will assist all of us in our further preparation:

1) Understand that everyone will experience the feelings of insecurity.
2) God will perform His will in and through our lives.
3) Two good verses to bring all of us in close are Proverbs 3:5–6.
4) Support the weak among us, those who are still struggling.
5) Pray daily for inner strength and confidence of mind.
6) Rejoice with those who have experienced progress in the move or in the stay.
7) Allow others to share their concerns in confidence. Apprehensions, joys, advances, problems, and challenges must be shared. Some may choose to do this privately, others publicly.
8) Keep ourselves in the scriptures daily.
9) Avoid a critical spirit toward circumstances or people. If it comes, confess it immediately before God.

10) Adjustments are easier for some than for others. Reach out to those who are not finding it easy.

11) Loneliness will be the experience of some. This is seldom expressed, but it will be there.

12) Change intimidates a few and challenges the Christian character of all. These changes will help us identify with our missionaries who flow down this river constantly.

13) Moving is taxing physically and emotionally. One of our missionaries recently stated to me that they had moved 34 times during their missionary career!

14) Staying will feel more comfortable, but you also will suffer loss. Prepare yourselves. Stay busy. Pray earnestly for this entire project. God will honor you for your spirit.

15) Watch out for the devil. The evil one will seek to impede your progress. Seek daily to possess the mind of Christ.

16) Read Philippians 2:1–5 daily. These verses will help for the journey ahead.

17) Make a personal list of those who you know need special attention in our prayers. Carry the list with you.

18) Uprooting from your church home will be traumatic. Locating another church where you feel comfortable will also stretch you. Remember how low Christ became when He reached out to us? We, like Him, can have a ministry of reaching out in the Harrisburg area.

19) Building programs, relocations, stays, transitions, and change can be the best times in our lives. A lot depends on what we make out of it. Don't let Satan take advantage of us during these times of opportunity for spiritual growth.

20) Take time to love one another. The best way to do this is through acts of kindness."

*Jeffrey Dragas  Skip Miller  Bernie Campbell  Myron Bieber  Frank Chambers  Frank Wilson  Carl Rietman  Ed Brown  Dave Holloway*

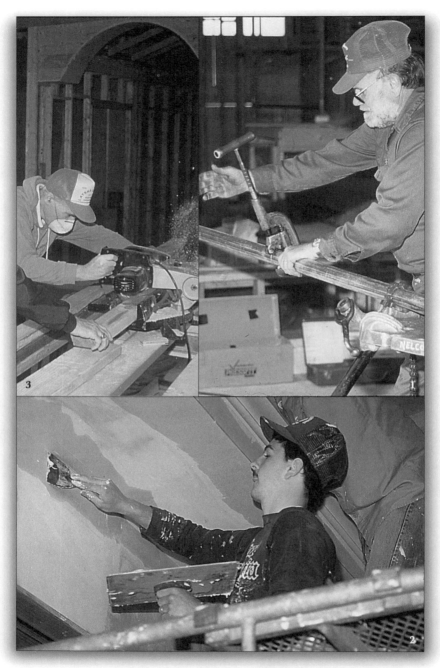

1–3. Finish work included trim work, painting and dry-walling.

# Light at the End
# of the Tunnel

As spring turned into summer, North Americans became involved in school graduations, weddings, and vacations. Fewer volunteers had signed up to work during the summer months, a time that was critical to completion of the project. Wendell Kempton send out a special letter to 1,596 pastors in a six-state area. He appealed for general laborers, carpenters, plumbers, painters, chain saw crews, dry wall finishers, electricians, and carpet layers. He said, "Please pray that a good number will respond. Frankly, we had not anticipated that the summer months would bring a lull. We are trusting the Lord to bring a bumper crop of volunteers during the months of June, July and August. Lord willing, we plan to celebrate the finished project on Labor Day."

An air of excitement pervaded the July board meetings when the president reported, "Already, more than 845 volunteers from 27 states and three foreign countries have worked on the project, saving us more than $1 million! Please continue to uphold Ralph and the team in your prayers. He and Evelyn have been instructed to take a giant rest in November and December after the project is done. Jay and Eleanor will be returning to Bangladesh. So far, Eleanor has been involved in serving over 11,000 meals. The Lord has put all of this

*Gene Falendysz   Bruce Ward   Mark Ward   Dave Irwin   Richard Post   Steve Sinkonis   Beryl Gow   Sally Schultz   David Ley   Mike Maliszewski*

together and only He will be able to properly reward His servants for their faithfulness."

In anticipation of the immediate future he said, "We are getting things ready to move the Cherry Hill operation to Harrisburg on September 8–10. A special ceremony is being planned for headquarters personnel on September 13–14. Continue to pray for our personnel. Twelve staff members have now sold their homes while nine others have not."

"There will be three dedication services," he added. "The first will be for our missionary family. Jay Walsh will bring the message on that occasion. This will be a fitting conclusion to the Missionary Enrichment Conference on Sunday, July 18. On Labor Day weekend a special dedication service will be held for the volunteers. Then on October 13–14 a dedication will be held for board members and dignitaries."

The appeal for more volunteers worked well for July and part of August. Ralph was pleased to report, "Last week we had the largest number of volunteers since the beginning of the work. This was a great encouragement to Dave Purrington and me. They accomplished an awful lot of work! Then, on Saturday, a new crew of 40 volunteers came, 32 from Colonial Baptist Church in Roanoke, Virginia, and eight from Heritage Baptist Church in Clark's Summit. God willing, we plan to bring the project to completion the last week of August. I know you have been praying, so this is certainly a note of praise!"

As August faded into history Wendell Kempton sent the following prayer requests to the board: "This is a hurried note to give you an update regarding the project. Please join in praying for the following: VOLUNTEERS NEEDED FOR THE FINAL PUSH. Please keep praying for Ralph, Jay, and Eleanor. This week and next week we are slim on volunteers. In the past three weeks great advances have been made. Three-quarters of the carpeting was laid last week. Ask God to direct to us those men and women needed for this vital, finish-construction stage."

Because of complications with occupancy permits, cou-pled with pending finish work, the move from Cherry Hill was postponed until September 22–24. Wendell said, "Our first official work days in the new facility will be September 27 and 28. These first two days together with our present staff and the new people joining us will be very important. We want a good beginning."

He then projected, "LABOR DAY VOLUNTEER DEDICATION . . . the number of those attending could go up to 450. They are coming in from all over the country. There seems to be a great spirit of enthusiasm. We will have a pig and chicken roast, supervised by Bob Hammaker. Pray for Dan Gelatt as he brings the dedication message for that occasion."

The final days of the project were a hum of activity as the volunteers, including the staff, pitched in to put the finishing touches to the building. The rotunda windows were washed, carpets vacuumed, walls decorated, and flowers ordered for the Labor Day dedication.

*Ruth Fluharty  Jane Garnham  Al Schultz  Dick Benshoof  Bob McLellan  Paul Snepp  Chuck Patton  Thomas Romeyn  Rob Kirby  Floyd Hardy*

1–3. Construction supervisors David Greening, Jerry VanHorne, and David Purrington.
4. "The blizzard of '93" dumped snow that had to be cleared out of the construction site.
5. Jay demonstrates being snowed in.

# The Three
# Superintendents

Moses' father-in-law, Jethro, gave him good advice one day. In so many words, Jethro said, "The work is too heavy for you: You cannot handle it alone. Select capable men from the people, men who fear God, trustworthy men, and appoint them. That will make your load lighter, because they will share it with you" (Exodus 18:18–22, paraphrased).

Ralph fully understood this biblical principle when he began the volunteer recruiting process. The Lord had men already picked out: Dave Greening from Muncy Valley, Pennsylvania; Jerry VanHorne from Rochester, New York; and Dave Purrington from Wheelersburg, Ohio. Those three men each invested months of their time on the project. Let's hear what these special men of God have to say:

## David Greening

Dave was God's man to supervise the first phase of the project. He knew how to operate heavy equipment and lay foundations that would stand the test of time. Here is is his testimony.

"One Sunday morning in the Bible Baptist Church of Huntersville, Pennsylvania, Wendell Kempton enlightened our congregation about the work and ministry of ABWE and their plans to build at a new location. After the service I asked him if there was any way I could participate in the construction process. At his suggestion, I made contact with Ralph Gruenberg, the project engineer, and later made a physical inspection of the site.

"I stood amazed at the beauty of the property God had graciously provided. Realizing that we would have to restructure the whole estate with volunteer help brought a little fear, not having tackled a job just like this before. Over a dinner table on the grounds, we talked about how we envisioned the new office complex and the physical changes on the mountain that would be made as the year ticked away.

"Bill Pierson, who I believe had a mysterious financial hand in the ongoing work, made my decision to become a part of this venture an easy task. Though I felt insufficient and weak to tackle such a job, I was reminded that God often uses 'the weak to confound the wise.' As long as God gets the glory, that is all that is important.

"From the start I saw God's hand at work. Men and women from all parts of the country showed up to give of their precious time to work so that the gospel of Christ would continue to reach all parts of the world. Willmer Stilwell from Washington proved to be one of the hardest workers. A retired mason, Connie DeRuyter, was full of vim and vigor. A young man from Ohio, Randy Riegsecker, drove the Bobcat faster than the speed of sound. The dynamite crew, led by Ziggy, excited the crowd when the ground bubbled and smoked. He was so good at his job, he told me, that I could stand at the corner of one of those explosions and not get hurt. My faith was weak and I kept way back with the rest of the spectators. I respected the fellow who drilled the holes for the charges because, at the end of the day, he was covered from head to foot with dust and looked like a ghost.

"I got to see pastors hit their fingers and keep their cool. I have special memories of having a word of prayer with a brother in the middle of a trying day, rejoicing at the sound of humming praises to the Lord, praying from time to time for God's wisdom, greeting my fellow workers with a smile and a word of encouragement. Oh how each day was filled with things for which to praise His dear name. Even when Ray Gerow was seriously injured, the presence of God's Spirit comforted and uplifted.

"Yes, for nearly five months I enjoyed working with some of God's finest saints. The ladies who made the meals, sharing their secret recipes, kept us strong and plump. The short Bible studies were encouraging, and Jay Walsh with his harmonica brought warmth to our singing. The muddy days with garbage bags for boots made us respect the dining hall a little more.

"Bulldozers and land movers of all sorts, with men who knew how to run them, etched out the ground, establishing the base for the foundations and a new road up the hill. The men laying cement blocks and rebar were hard at work in different sections. The groups were yelling out, 'More mud, please!'— all at the same time. Then the concrete trucks climbed into almost impossible positions as we filled the cavities in the blocks, pouring footers and floors. It was exciting to share Christ with the various vendors as they unloaded their goods.

"I remember the motel where most of us stayed, four to a room. Most of the guys snored, but we were too tired to pay much attention. Each day presented new challenges, but God's grace was good. Looking back, there were times when my attitude needed improvement, when my zeal lost its luster. But I thank God for the opportunity He gave me. Some day, Lord willing, I may have another chance to serve Him in a project like this."

Dave was saved at seven years of age at an evangelistic service in Saugerties, New York. At that meeting he realized he was lost and bound for an eternity without God. He accepted the Lord Jesus Christ as his personal Savior and con-

Darin Stevens  Dan Wyma  Don Remer  Kim Lewis  Dick Wyma  Walter Schmidt, Jr.  Donna Schmidt  Matt Clouse  Greg Heath  Dennis Tubbs

tinues to be humbly grateful to God for His unspeakable gift. Dave shared some of his life's principles.

1) Labor each day as if it were your last.
2) Chart life's course with care, or you'll drift forever.
3) Smile in the face of adversity until it surrenders.
4) Never forget, it's always later than you think.
5) Separate yourself from the crowd; don't just be a nibbling sheep.
6) Go the extra mile; always give more than is expected.
7) There is a seed of good in every adversity; God closes one door and opens another.
8) Don't neglect the little things; even small work is important.
9) Don't hide behind busy work; do what is important, not what is urgent. Time is our most precious possession. Use it wisely.
10) Never allow anyone to rain on your parade; criticism and envy from others can wound your inner self. Smile and go on. At the end of the journey, God will be smiling.

Dave's Christian philosophy of life showed through during his time on the project. Those who worked with him will never forget his contribution to the project and God's Kingdom.

## Gerald VanHorne

Dave's departure in December 1992 opened the way for the VanHornes in early January. Jerry and Florence are members of the North Baptist Church in Rochester, New York, where Ralph and Evelyn had pastored before joining ABWE. Jerry recalls the time when Ralph and other church families helped on a missions project in The Gambia. Because he was working full time, Jerry couldn't go. Nonetheless, having previously been involved with a number of projects in Canada, where he had once lived, Jerry was open to new opportunities as they came along. He shares the following testimony:

"About the time that Ralph Gruenberg resigned from North Baptist Church, he notified us of his alignment with ABWE. Soon thereafter he started circulating information to the church about the possibility of an upcoming project in which we could be involved. As more details became available, my enthusiasm began to rise. I filled out a volunteer form and waited to see what would develop.

"My wife and I planned a trip to North Carolina for a week's vacation in the spring of 1992. Ralph asked us to stop in Harrisburg where he and Evelyn were living. He said he wanted to show me the plans of the proposed project. Little did I know what he was leading up to! At the end of our discussion he said, 'I plan on dividing the project into three segments.' It was then that he asked if I would consider being in charge of the second phase of construction. This was quite a shock to me, but also a tremendous compliment. I was thinking that I could help out for a couple of weeks when he added that it would be a three-month assignment, and would involve both Florence and me. Now I was hooked!

"We left for our vacation promising to pray about it and let him know of our decision when we returned. Our minds were in a whirl the entire week. Because we had strong feelings of wanting to do the Lord's will and His work, we gave Ralph our answer: Yes, we are willing, and with God's help we'll do our best.

"Looking back, my experience on the project was unique in so many ways. ABWE supplied a lovely ranch home on the premises where Florence and I lived comfortably (except for a number of sleepless nights thinking about the project).

"We were on the mountain for a total of about four months. Those were special days filled with wonderful memories. I believe the most enjoyable times were our morning devotions before starting work. Some days, with the pressure of the work at hand, and time seemingly at a premium, one would almost automatically feel that a short prayer would do. However, with Jay's God-given talent of leadership, his special way of directing those times, and his harmonica playing, the pressure valve automatically began releasing. We were wafted into a new spiritual realm of calmness as testimonies were given and experiences shared. It was not unusual to see tears flowing, and, when finished, we felt we could conquer the world.

"Each Monday morning we met so many strangers, and on Friday night we had an emotional farewell as our new-found brothers and sisters in Christ had to leave. I still get choked up thinking back on those wonderful times. They supersede the ankle-deep mud, gale force winds, and knee-high snowdrifts.

"How can we forget the wonderful meals that Eleanor and the ladies, including my wife, Florence, prepared for us? The homemade sticky buns and bread. God was so good!"

Jerry was raised in a Christian home in Picton, Ontario, Canada. He attended a church that believed a person could lose salvation. As a teenager he became disenchanted and confused, losing interest in church. About six years later he married Florence, a Methodist, and began attending her church. One day, a circuit-riding Baptist minister called on the couple. As a result of that man's ministry, Jerry and Florence accepted Christ as Lord and Savior, realizing it was a once-for-all decision. Jerry confidently testifies, "We can go to sleep now realizing if we aren't perfect, the Lord forgives. With His help and our asking for forgiveness, we can look forward to the day when we all meet in heaven. Praise the Lord!"

During Jerry's tenure of service, the auditorium and rotunda areas were completed and covered. Most of the electric, computer, and phone lines had been strung and much of the insulation and dry wall installed. Jerry and Florence left the project on April 30, 1993. The Lord provided great teams of workers during Jerry's tenure, which was interrupted by what the local newspaper called "the storm of the century." It rolled in on the evening of March 12 and blew itself out three days later, leaving behind four feet of snow!

## David Purrington

Like the old adage "He who laughs last, laughs best," our adage is "He who comes last, works longest." Five days before the VanHornes left on April 30, 1993, Dave arrived on the project and ended up staying until the volunteer dedication on Labor Day. Dave shares his story:

"While I was living in Wheelersburg, Ohio, and attending Wheelersburg Baptist Church, information regarding the ABWE building project in Harrisburg was shared during one of the services. Since I am a builder, that announcement stirred my interest. I decided, along with some of the other men in the church, to help with the construction for two weeks. I returned my volunteer registration form and left the timing with the Lord.

"In June 1992, Ralph Gruenberg made a special trip to Indiana and Ohio to meet with prospective volunteer groups that had indicated an interest in the project. After Ralph learned that I was an experienced carpenter, he asked if I would consider supervising the project for the final stages of construction [what Dave did not realize is that Ralph had already checked out his background, and inspected some of his earlier work at Cedarville College, according to Ralph.] His proposal now became more of a family decision because of the length of time I would be away from home. I discussed this with Pamela, my wife, and Derek, our son. With their encouragement I accepted the job for the months of June and July.

"In November, just before Thanksgiving, Pam and I drove to Harrisburg to see the project site firsthand. This gave

*Sonya Peace  Larry Lee  Lauerane Lee  Brian Michael  Bob Olson  Carl Olson  Carolyn Balko  Ruth Lee  Nate Gentry  David Parmerlee*

me an idea of the size of the job and what I might face when I arrived in June. As the weeks passed, I kept in touch with Ralph regarding the building progress. Each time I talked with him he asked if I could come sooner. Being self-employed allowed me to adjust my schedule. So in the last week of April 1993, I left Wheelersburg for Harrisburg with a borrowed car and a U-Haul trailer loaded with tools. I had only five days to learn from Jerry before he left on April 30. Little did I realize at the time that I would carry the ball, not for just two months, but until the dedication of the completed building in September.

"Looking back on those days, I will never forget the sensitivity of Dr. Kempton and others who made it possible for Pam and Derek to be with me on the job. I had the special opportunity of working with Ralph Gruenberg. His excitement and commitment to the project challenged and encouraged me as we dealt with all kinds of situations that arose while working with willing volunteers, some of whom had no construction experience at all.

"I was greatly impressed with the team spirit. The project was accomplished with much sacrifice and many long hours of work. Everyone responded with positive and supportive efforts. Even when fatigue seemed to be taking over, the volunteers were willing to 'go the extra mile.'

"Each day before setting out, we had a time of devotions together. What special times of blessing and encouragement they were to me. On numerous occasions we construction workers, some facing major adversities and unspoken personal burdens, shed tears together as we sang hymns and shared testimonies.

"What a challenge it was every Monday morning after devotions for me to organize the new crew of volunteers who had arrived for the week. We had to find the right slots for them and by the end of the week everybody worked together like clockwork. The Lord led each of these volunteers who

*Robert Strope  Almeeda Strope  Marie Andreasen  Art Andreasen  Ron Gentry  Bill Pippinger  Carol Pippinger  Frank Butterfield  Anna Butterfield*

made the 'miracle on the hill' possible: Tom and Marilyn Royal from West Unity, Ohio; Sam and Lilly Wiseman from York, Pennsylvania; Art and Marie Eshleman from Binghamton, New York; Willmer (Will) Stilwell from Lynnwood, Washington; Frank and Anna Butterfield from Lapeer, Michigan; the Jertberg father-and-sons team from Florida; big Randy Riegsecker, a college student from Stryker, Ohio; Matthew Walsh (Jay and Eleanor's grandson) from Dover, Delaware; Ken and Sue James from Mishawaka, Indiana; Dave Ruffer from Stryker, Ohio; and Bill and Carol Pepperidge from Grand Rapids, Michigan (he fell from the scaffolding and broke his leg), are just a few people I will never forget. The Lord used them in my life, through their abilities, their humor, and their commitment."

Dave came to know Christ after living what he describes as a "selfish life," when he allowed the things of this world to control him. During a year of separation from Dave, Pam came to know the Lord through some literature from Campus Crusade for Christ. She began attending a Baptist church and Dave watched these developments, all the while saying to himself, "I could never do anything like that." As Dave puts it, "A year and several trips to church with Pam later, the Lord used a missionary and a pastor, each with construction backgrounds, to first share 2 x 4's before talking to me about John 3:16. Wisely, they didn't try to cram religion down my throat, but let me know that they were common, ordinary people who knew how to saw lumber and pound nails."

Attracted to the Christian life by those faithful witnesses, Dave trusted in Christ as His personal Savior and lives now by his life verses, Proverbs 3:5–6: "Trust in the Lord with all thine heart; and lean not unto thine own understanding. In all thy ways acknowledge him, and he shall direct thy paths."

1. Volunteers return. 2. ABWE president emeritus Dr. Harold T. Commons.
3. Sign greeting guests. 4. Special speaker Jack Wyrtzen. 5., 6., 9. Ralph thanks the volunteers.
7., 8., Special guests Joe Gibbs and Lt. Gov. Mark Singel.

*Lorraine McHargue  George Sun  Lanney McHargue  Kyle McHargue  Lynn Talbot  Karen Cooper  Phyllis Smith  Ernie Stover  Jan Robinson*

# A Time for Celebrating

Dedication day, September 5, 1993, dawned sunny and bright. Huge tents filled the parking lot. A big cardboard sign hung by a volunteer on a crane at the parking lot entrance proclaimed: IT'S A MIRACLE! Approximately 450 volunteers and their families read that sign as they drove up the hill to celebrate the "miracle on the hill."

The physical food was fabulous and the spiritual food and fellowship that followed was heavenly. The crowd joined in singing the project theme song, *Savior Like A Shepherd Lead Us*, as Jay once more played his harmonica. Wendell Kempton honored Ralph for his leadership in the project. He also honored his aged father who contributed financially to the project and attended the ceremony. When Harvey Kempton took the microphone he said to the volunteers with a twinkle in his eye, "President Lincoln freed the slaves, but it's obvious that Wendell hasn't learned that lesson yet." We roared with laughter.

After the honors and acknowledgments were over and after we feasted on roast pork and chicken, we stood for a final prayer. Pastor Chesford Carr of Emmanuel Baptist Church in Mechanicsburg, Pennsylvania, thanked our heavenly Father for the miracle on the hill, now a vision fulfilled. As evening shadows approached, the volunteers said their farewells and drifted away with memories never to be forgotten. God, indeed, had accomplished His perfect will.

By the end of September the Walshes and Purringtons had returned to their homes in Michigan and Ohio. The Cherry Hill staff had taken up their posts in the new facilities. On October 4 Wendell Kempton informed the board, "The MIRACLE continues! All personnel, all the furniture, and all the boxes arrived from Cherry Hill. Our official office opening was Monday, September 27. God gave us a wonderful beginning with two days of getting to know one another. Russ Ebersole challenged us from the Word of God. We listened to some beautiful testimonies, learned about one another, and talked together about what the future holds for ABWE. Thank you for praying. What an encouragement that has been!"

October 13 and 14 will go down in the history of the ABWE as two dynamite days with the board and staff. On the 13th, before a crowd of 200 people, Ralph expressed his thanks to all who assisted in the project. He proudly said, "The volunteer concept has worked. It worked because God worked. More than 1,100 volunteers have come from 27 states, Canada, Bermuda, Wales, Hungary, the Philippines, and Togo to help. Many of those were teenagers and retired people. Many people gave gifts of materials and supplies and some helped pay for contractual work to be done."

President Kempton shared statistics comparing the cost to complete the project with volunteer labor versus contracted labor. "With volunteers we built at a cost of $46 per square foot. Had the project been done commercially, the figure would have been between $95 and $105 per square foot!"

In the same meeting tribute was paid to Dr. Harold T. Commons, former ABWE president, and Rev. Edward C. Bomm, former ABWE missionary and treasurer, as two sec-

*Raymond Jones  Debby Jones  Allen Webster  Tim Eichner  Jerry Montgomery  Daneen Campbell  Gary Campbell  Claudia Austin*

tions of the building were named in their honor. The administration wing would be known in the future as the Commons Administrative Center and the financial wing as the Edward Bomm Financial Center. Board members then divided into two groups for prayer followed by a tour of the new building. That evening they gathered for dinner and a celebration of praise. After giving special recognition to the Gruenbergs, Walshes, and Piersons for their tireless work throughout the project, the evening was capped off with a challenge from Jack Wyrtzen. It was, indeed, a time for rejoicing.

About the special events of October 14 Wendell wrote, "We welcomed acting Pennsylvania Governor Mark Singel to lunch and presented him with a new Bible. Many other dignitaries joined us, along with the area business people and vendors who had a part in the 'miracle on the hill.' Pastor and Mrs. Randy Gaumer of Perkasie, Pennsylvania, favored us with special music. Then Joe Gibbs, former head coach of the Washington Redskins football team, addressed the more than 250 assembled. He hit the mark by giving his personal testimony with a clear presentation of the gospel, emphasizing the importance of a personal relationship with Jesus. He concluded his testimony by giving an open invitation to receive Christ as Savior."

On the day of this third and final dedication God sent in an unsolicited gift of $200,000. The "miracle on the hill" was completed debt-free. The miraculous journey, covering months of planning and hard work, was now over and the face of ABWE, as predicted by their leader, would never again be the same. To God be the glory; great things He has done!

*Delores Montgomery  Bob Austin, Sr.  Ronald Kelbett  Michael Cushman  Anna Clark  Dwight Clark  Frank Jertberg  Timothy Jertberg*

1. Eleanor Walsh and Sharon Hammaker, chief cooks.  2. Volunteers eating one of 13,000 meals served.  3. Betty Tideman, volunteer cook.

*Thomas Jertberg  Terry Jertberg  Howard Fyock  Tim Mundinger  Fred Brownlee  Tony Oldham  Dale Bieber  Scott Roach  Joe Scotto*

# Parade of Cooks

The volunteers were responsible for their own room and board, and at least eight hours a day of hard work. In one of his now-famous volunteer bulletins Ralph said, "My guess is that it's going to be cheaper to eat here than at home, unless you still live with your mother!"

The manager of the Knights Inn in New Cumberland graciously agreed to allow up to four men to stay in a room for only $25 a day. ABWE provided a daily lunch, dinner, and two coffee breaks for $5. With that slim budget, the Walshes managed to feed more than 1,100 volunteers over a period of 14 months. Before the project was over, 13,000 meals and an equal number of coffee breaks had been served.

Sharon Hammaker carried the food responsibilities at the outset of the project until IBM transferred her husband, Bob, to Colorado on temporary assignment. With Sharon gone, Eleanor assumed full responsibility for the meals and depended on the help of many ladies. Weeks later, after Sharon returned, she again played a major role by assisting with food purchasing and giving Eleanor a much-appreciated day off each week.

There is a saying that "many cooks spoil the broth," but that rarely happened. We will never forget all the special women who came from far and near to share their time and recipes. To record their names here is not possible and, if we tried, we would surely miss someone. The Lord knows each one and He has kept an accurate record. ABWE salutes each of them.

This account would not be complete, however, unless we shared some of the more memorable stories that centered around special people. For weeks Eleanor made bread and cinnamon buns, kneading the dough by hand, until Charlene Gartin from Des Moines, Iowa, arrived on the scene. Charlene brought with her a Bosch bread mixer, a wonderful addition to the kitchen gadgetry. Later, with her encouragement, Eleanor appealed successfully to the "powers that be" and purchased the machine when Charlene left. After that, bread-making became a pleasure, not a chore, and the workers benefited greatly. If the men had to choose between a bulldozer or a bread mixer, to a man they would choose the latter!

Samuel and Lilly Wiseman from York, Pennsylvania, contributed as much or more time to the miracle on the hill than any other couple. Lilly became Eleanor's "right-hand man," and they became the best of friends. Not only did Lilly help in the preparation of meals, she knew how to find food bargains, especially meats. In her earlier years she had worked in a meat market and learned what cuts to buy and where to find the best prices. Because of Lilly's expertise, the women put terrific meals on the table at a greatly reduced cost.

Bill and Jan Wemett from Rochester, New York, worked on the project at different times. Jan decided one day to brew a kettle of her famous "Everything-But-The-Kitchen-Sink Soup." That two-day process required Eleanor getting up in the middle of the night to stir it! The soup was great, and the crew raved about it.

Frequently there were leftovers. A common question to Eleanor was, "What shall we do with these leftovers?" To which she would reply, "Put them in the freezer." One day when Eleanor was digging in the freezer she found a 3 x 5 card tucked into a tin on which was written: "Thanks for a wonderful week in the kitchen. It couldn't have been better. We'll always remember your words of wisdom, 'put it in the freezer,' so we did!" The card was signed by Mary Parmerlee, Pam Purrington, Marilyn Jarrard, Sue James, Sharon Hammaker, and Carole Beverly.

Ray and Priscilla LaBonte from Wisconsin also worked on the project. One day Priscilla suggested to Eleanor that she compile a cookbook with recipes contributed by the volunteers. Eleanor began collecting favorite recipes. Towards the end of the project Nancy LaBonte typed most of them into Jay's computer, a painstaking task. Later someone accidentally hit the wrong key and erased the whole thing! Carol and Kristen Stagg came to the rescue, retyped the recipes and, after the Walshes returned to Bangladesh, published *Recipes From Miracle Mountain.* The cover was designed by Marilyn Royal, a volunteer and glass etcher from West Unity, Ohio.

The dedication says: "This book of recipes is dedicated to all the ladies who assisted in the preparation of over 13,000 meals during the construction of ABWE's new international headquarters near Harrisburg, Pennsylvania. THANK YOU to the more than 1,100 volunteers, including the kitchen assistants, who donated their time and talents from August 1992 to September 1993 to the 'Miracle on the Mountain.' "

Eleanor received many encouraging notes from the volunteers after they returned home:

"I loved being with you last week. It was a privilege to be able to work with the ladies in the kitchen. Isn't it great how knowing the Lord gives us an instant bond with other believers? You have a special gift for making people feel comfortable. Thanks for your kindness to me. It was fun working with you. Hope the pumpkin pie turned out okay!"

*John Wulfing  Flobie Fel Escobar  Josie Ann Zamar  Cristine Negosa  Zinnia Zamar  Edwin Du  Nenita Nifras  Raquel Polec-Eo*

"Just wanted to say thanks for going out of your way to care for us."

"Thank you for your help and Godly witness."

"What's cooking this week? I hope you have plenty of help. I really can't express how much my week at ABWE meant. God certainly knew what I needed that week: the fellowship I've been starving for with other Christian women. It has definitely been the highlight of my summer. Believe it or not, I returned home with renewed energy and wasn't tired."

"I made six loaves of bread this afternoon. Yes, I'm still at it. Sometimes I long for that bread mixer we had at Harrisburg. Eleanor, the time I spent in the kitchen there with you was so special. I'll never forget those good sticky rolls and the hamburger rolls we laughed over. What a good time, and what precious fellowship. What a great Lord we have to make so many sweet people who love Him. Wherever we go there are some more."

"It was great working with you this past week. I learned so much from you, Eleanor!"

"Brrr! It is cold in North Carolina this morning. We trust that the workmen are making good progress. Trust these pans will come in handy in your kitchen as you feed those hungry men. We think back with pleasure to our week with you."

"I've enjoyed my time there, but, Eleanor, I don't know how you can do it for a year!" (Lolita Barram after she and John covered for the Walshes while they made a short trip to Bangladesh in December 1992.)

"It's me—the lady roofer! Just a note to say you are a very sweet lady. Our weeks with you were great. You make everyone feel so wanted and at home. I just wish I could have given you a better good-bye than I did. You deserved a huge hug. I hope the Lord will allow us to come back. It was so good working with the people of God instead of ones of the world."

The men also appreciated the kitchen crew:

"Homemade bread and biscuits, homemade pies and pizzas, turkey dinners, Bangladeshi and Burmese curries, gigantic subs, hefty bean soup, baked chicken, goulash, you name it—we've had it. Where else can you feast like this for only $5 a day?"

"Thanks for all your hosting care for us. The know-how of the culinary department was great. When 12:00 and 5:30 hours came there was a tantalizing aroma and a delicious meal for us ravenous workers!"

"It brings real joy to remember the times at the building project and the spiritual emphasis that drew us all together. My, how God did bless! One day we will be able to rehearse those times together and rejoice again at the miracles that God performed at Harrisburg."

The contribution to the "miracle on the hill" by women cannot be overestimated. Ralph summed it up nicely when he wrote, "I can't say enough about the kitchen crew and about what their work has meant to us all. Nor can I fully appreciate the burden those valiant ladies carried in the continual, daily food planning and preparation. Their labor has been just as essential as any roofer's or carpenter's. I salute them."

How true! The women provided a dimension of expertise that made the volunteer story a huge success.

Ernst Hartline  Ralph Flynn  Adam Fridstrom  Derek Purrington  Pamela Purrington  Domer Zerbe  Harry Suplee  Larry Cauffman

1. Dwight Clark, WWII veteran.  2. One of the teen volunteers.  3. Volunteer from Wales.
4. Frank Butterfield.  5. The Bronkemas.  6. Volunteer contingent from
Bible Baptist Church, Shiremanstown.

*Eric Dillworth  Bill Dillworth  Dave Bechtel  DeElda Payton  Bernard Beverly  David Minium  John Lowrey  Steve Kingsley  Jim Knobloch*

# Volunteer Hall of Fame

O n November 1, 1993, Ralph and Evelyn Gruenberg sat together looking at project photos. Evelyn commented, "Those guys really worked!" In his last volunteer letter Ralph wrote, "The pictures caused us to relive the amazing past 15 months. They evoked memories of the 1,140 people who came here to be a part of the miracle. The pictures weren't people all dressed and posed for a portrait. They were images of men working in mud and snow, handing up materials, operating equipment, measuring, and eating. Women painting, cooking, baking, serving. Yes, honey, those 'guys' really worked." Charles Haddon Spurgeon couldn't have said it more eloquently.

In an earlier bulletin Ralph had told the volunteers, "Wait till you get here. You will never see weeks speed by as quickly as they do on this hilltop. I've tried to analyze why. I think it's three factors:

- No boredom. No time for it.
- No routine. No rut. The scenery and the work are constantly changing.
- The people you work with. You enjoy their company.

"You'll see what I mean when you get here. The hours are long, but the weeks are short. You wouldn't believe the hours some of our volunteers insist on. You can't hold them down. They are here to work, and believe me, they do. But still, the weeks are short, and the farewells we say every Friday and Saturday come all too quickly.

"When I watch what's happening I often think of Nehemiah chapter 3. Those recurring phrases *'next to him,'* and *'next to them.'* That's how Jerusalem's wall was rebuilt. Each person, each group doing a part, while God shaped their labor into a unified, integrated, amazing whole.

"I think about the names in Nehemiah 3. Most aren't recorded anywhere else. Only in God's private book. It will be that way with us, too. Twenty years from now few will remember that a **Bob Beikert** or a **Phil Smith** or a **Debra Daam** was here, and who it was that worked next to them. That's all right. We're not here to be noticed. We're here to serve the Lord and His people and to do our small part so that God can be glorified in a finished, functional mission and training center. I will do everything to help make your investment of time and effort really count. In a sense, what you are investing is even more precious than money. That's because you are investing a slice of life itself."

Like the unsung heroes of faith in Hebrews 11, we also had many who invested a slice of their lives. **Jane Garnam** was the first volunteer on the project. **Dana Steele,** a junior civil engineering student, helped survey the lines and grades on the road and structures. The **Marsh family: Robert, Laura, Gary,** and **Robert Jr.,** played a significant part. Bob Sr. supervised the entire earth-moving operation. **Bill Pisch,** a willing laborer, lived with his dog in a pup tent on the hillside. **James Wilson** donated several weeks of time and, two years later in 1995, died unexpectedly from a brain hemorrhage.

**Wyman Ritchie,** a finish carpenter, skillfully removed two built-in mirrored china cabinets and later reinstalled them (he also got temporarily lost under the flooring of the original building while working on a fire barrier wall. Someone had to thump the floor to guide him to the exit). **Ken Hunt,** a roofing contractor from Ontario, Canada, helped tremendously with the roofing. **Laurens Richard,** who worked as a mason tender for Sam Wiseman ("The best one I ever had," says Sam), gave 10 weeks of his time. **Meryl and Beryl Dornan,** twin brothers from Twinsburg, Ohio, operated twin roller compactors on the parking lot. **Ted Walborn,** one of the oldest volunteers, who came despite serious heart problems, left his fingerprints on the brooms while keeping the construction areas clean of sawdust and debris.

How can we adequately thank **Paul Liskey** or **Randy Riegsecker** for their extended service? Randy, a college student, loved to operate the heavy equipment. **Dean Rypkema** of the Nelcorp Company and "super" **Herb Olmstead,** electrical superintendent, not only installed the complex electrical system but charmed us with his wit and humor. **Larry Bach** designed the complex electric service switch gear and walked it through all the power company's approvals. Pastors **Paul Sears** and **Ray Garthwaite,** both having had previous construction experience, worked on the job.

The Kempton Karpenters (from Wendell's home church in Iowa): **Art Cross, Garret Loverink, Delbert Feldman, Kevin Pals,** and **John Carlson** advanced the project considerably. The five Minnesota natives, **Ted Weinberg, Al Schultz, Dick Benshoof, Bob McLellan,** and **Chuck Patton,** thought Harrisburg's cold weather during the most bitter week of the entire project was warm, and threw off their jackets to work. (Ted later became an ABWE career missionary.) Retired missionaries **John and Lolita Barram** covered for the Walshes while they were in

Bangladesh. The three generational family **Mr. and Mrs. Austin Trimble, Ray and Priscilla LaBonte,** and **Nancy LaBonte** (ABWE appointee to South Africa at the time) showed up several times.

**Tom and Marilyn Royal,** members of the carpenter crew, nailed shingles on the roof. Marilyn also had another talent. All the glass etchings in the building are her contribution. **Derek Purrington,** a budding teenage graphics designer, trimmed the conference rooms to perfection.

Repeat volunteers like **Bill Brungard, Bob Hammaker,** and **Jon Delavan** played significant roles in making the miracle come true. **Dwight Clark,** the Carolina painter, told us stories of WWII when he helped rescued ABWE internees at the Los Baños prison camp in the Philippines. Those paratroopers delivered Mona Kemery, Ruth Woodworth, and the Henry DeVries family from execution on February 23, 1945. **Frank and Anna Butterfield** made their marks on the project. Frank lost his hand in a corn chopper in 1970 but that didn't stop him. He made an artificial hand with an attached hammer and pounded in nails like the two-armed carpenters around him. **Bob Cooper,** representing First Baptist Church of Bellefonte, Pennsylvania, and head of their Men For Missions ministry, brought over 60 volunteers at different times during the course of the project.

**Audrey Aviet, Martin and Sue Walsh,** and **Don Love** pushed paintbrushes and rollers to make the finished product even more attractive. Mason and concrete finisher **Kurt Sager** returned again and again. The rear entrance steps represent part of his handiwork. **Bob Clifton** from Marion, Ohio, took charge of stringing more than 27 miles of wire throughout the buildings. ABWE's director of information systems, **Paul Sturgis,** made 56 round trips between Cherry Hill and Harrisburg during the installation of telephone and computer lines and equipment. **Richard**

*Christine Herring  Fred Herring  Cara Tavella  Natalia O'Brien  Rebecca Southwell  Andy Dietz  Patricia O'Brien  Pete Hoghansen  Jabe Thomas*

**Phelps, Leo Custodio,** and **Bill Parmerlee,** all men of means, labored and perspired along with the rest.

Electrician **John Geshay** and his wife, **Gladys,** continued to send Danish pastries from Racine, Wisconsin, after they left the project. **Forest and Iva Swineford,** after donating their time on the project, felt called to short-term missions in the Philippines. **Dan Baker,** the rugged, full-bearded nurseryman from Berkshire, New York, often appeared to check on the health of the transplanted shrubs. His expert care and management of plants and trees was a big help.

And, how can we forget to mention a local dry-waller who moonlighted as a bartender in New Cumberland? This young man, who wouldn't record his name in the volunteer registry, not only worked on walls and ceilings but carried in leftover spaghetti sauce from the tavern for the cooks to use. Yes, a number of non-Christians volunteered, too!

The list goes on a thousand times over. There are countless fingerprints left on this building by choice servants of God who will go unheralded and unnamed, except by our great Architect and Builder in Heaven. The volunteers came from other construction projects, but also from mission fields, classrooms, factories, farms, and offices. Military men, commissioned and non-commissioned officers, volunteered while on leave from the Army, Air Force, and Coast Guard. Each contributed time, skills, and physical effort to complete a huge and awesome task. The nature of the project drew the interest of a York newspaper, *The Daily Record,* and Harrisburg's *The Patriot-News.* Both papers published articles about the project. The York paper's special article featured Sam Wiseman, who would never have sought that recognition, but deserved it.

In a special final letter to the volunteers, dated November 1, 1993, Wendell Kempton said, "Today, as I walked through this marvelous facility, I paused again to thank God for all the beautiful people who came to make it

David W. Cooper, Jr.   David W. Cooper   Dennis Rust   David Waters   Steve Aime   Matt Douglas   Ernie Reinertsen   Josh Reinertsen

possible. Praise God from whom all blessings flow. Great things He hath done." And, in a humbling tribute to the Gruenbergs and Walshes, he wrote, "The official board of ABWE, the staff, our missionaries around the world, and our volunteers desire to express sincerest appreciation. As couples you teamed up in leading the way. The project became a reality because you were willing to be obedient to God's leading in your lives. Your sacrifice and labors of love will not go unrewarded. Your contributions will serve to remind all of us that God has highly honored us through knowing you and serving along side you. We will forever be grateful for all that you have done to promote HIS KINGDOM."

The dedication monument in front of the mission appropriately reads: This property is dedicated to the glory of God, to the local churches and their missionaries with whom we labor in the worldwide proclamation of the gospel in accordance with the Great Commission (Matthew 28:19–20). We are grateful to the more than 1,100 volunteers from 27 states, Canada, Bermuda, Togo, Wales, Hungary, and the Philippines who gave sacrificially of their time and talents to construct this Administration Building and Training Center.

TO GOD BE THE GLORY. GREAT THINGS HE HATH DONE!

*Polly Hamilton   Peter Beck   Sue Hahn   Chris Bennetts   Ben Summerfield   Tom Storms   Dan Sensenbaugh   Robert Wazny   Chad Cragg   Liz Finzel*

*Miranda Holecheck  Patti Summerfield  Steve Summerfield  Anna Lee Raven  Morgan Mitchell  Sara Sensenbaugh  Paul Smith  Rachel Tabberer*

1. Front entrance to the building.  2. Rotunda.  3. Final landscaping at entryway.
4. Aerial view of completed construction.

*Kay Washer  Marilyn Jarrard  Brian Jarrard  Nance Reinertsen  Pat Waters  Fred Hering  Bill Bingman  John Austin  Larry Sanderson*

# Special Mention

Giving credit to those who deserve it is a biblical concept. God's Word encourages us to give honor to whom honor is due. Let's do it!

### Wendell & Ruth Kempton

Wendell was God's man to originate and orchestrate the move from Cherry Hill, New Jersey, to Harrisburg, Pennsylvania. In making that decision he bore the burden of funding the project and moving a staff that had long been rooted in the Cherry Hill area. His vision for the future of ABWE, his unwavering faith that he was moving in the will of God, and his godly life have impacted us all.

Ruth stood by Wendell's side praying for him and encouraging him. Early in the project this couple canceled a scheduled anniversary trip in order to operate tractor/compactors during road construction. In her unique way Ruth left her imprint on the project, not only through manual labor, but by her gifts for design and decoration. Every area of the new buildings evidence her handiwork.

## William & Betty Pierson

Bill was the backstage star of the
project. Only the official minutes of the
mission's many meetings over a three-
year period reveal that story. He was
responsible for the property search and
handled most of the sensitive negotiations that finally led ABWE to the

McKinney estate. Like the rock of Gibraltar, Bill stands firm
in his commitment to ABWE and his faith in Christ.

Betty was always present to carry out special mission
responsibilities, even when there might have been an easier
way out. Her faithful support of Bill throughout the several
years of the project has not passed unnoticed.

## Gary & Barbara Helsel

Gary played a major role in focus-
ing the ABWE leadership to consider
moving to the Harrisburg area. He had
shared some of the benefits and features
of the greater Harrisburg area with the
Kemptons and Piersons on October 10,
1989. Months later, when the Search
Committee decided to go there, Gary

put Wendell and Bill in touch with key people who would
become deeply involved in the move. When construction
started, Gary was appointed as the project clerk. He took on
the responsibility of establishing commercial credit with
numerous vendors throughout the area and tracking thousands of invoices and expenditures on a day-by-day basis.

Barbara became Ralph Gruenberg's construction office
secretary. He really needed her. She kept the volunteer
records and helped with many logistical aspects of the project.
We cannot forget this couple's investment in ABWE's move.

*Steven Clark   Richard Yorkel   Phil Kasper   Charles Moyer   Dorothy Dibble   John Bole   Elizabeth Bole   Ruth Bole   Rebekah Bole   David Daam*

### Evelyn Tworzydlo

With no fanfare at all, Evelyn Tworzydlo of the Cherry Hill staff was designated to do the secretarial work Ralph faxed from Harrisburg. This turned into a steady stream of letters, notes, and reports—hundreds of items that she handled with accuracy and  finesse. Eventually she typed and mailed the many volunteer bulletins that were sent worldwide.

### Michael McKinney

As the owner of Capitol View Manor and the 134.19 acre estate, Mike McKinney could have refused to sell his choice property. Instead, understanding and appreciating ABWE's vision for evangelism and church planting, and personally interested in humanitarian and religious causes, he sold his estate  for $1 million less than its appraised value. ABWE salutes Michael for his generosity and sacrifice.

### Mark & Nancy Nelson

Owner of the Nelcorp Company of Edwell, New York, Mark oversaw the design and installation of the electrical system in the buildings. This included the donation of electrical materials, and the provision of a Christian electrical superintendent. A dedicated Christian  businessman, Mark saw the bigger picture for accomplishing world evangelism, and acted accordingly. He and his wife, Nancy, have since sold their business and joined ABWE. They designed and led the teen Expedition ministry and are active in many facets of mission administrative work.

### Roger Petrone

Gary Helsel introduced Roger to ABWE. Several possible architects were interviewed before the design process got under way. Roger impressed Ralph for two reasons: his office was in nearby Camp Hill, Pennsylvania, and he was a believer who expressed to Ralph, "I have never had a chance to serve the Lord in this way." Roger donated all of his time for the project. His skillful management of the design process was key in expediting the permits that would have taken much longer than our schedule allowed. The beautiful and functional design of the buildings will always bear his mark.

### Kwang Kim

Mr. Kim is a Pennsylvania Power and Light Company electrical engineer. His influence in negotiating the special benefits and credits that ABWE received is remarkable. Mr. Kim is a Korean-American and a fellow believer in Christ, who enthusiastically supports ABWE's vision for world evangelism.

## Alvah & Anne Ehrman

Owners of Ehrman's Plumbing and Heating in Hamburg, New York, and dedicated Christians, this couple volunteered a special service that brought them back to Harrisburg many times before the project was completed. Al was in charge of the heating, ventilation, air conditioning (HVAC), and plumbing design and installation. He and Anne made weekly inspection trips, often in inclement weather, to make sure the volunteers and contractors installed the equipment correctly. Anne often assisted in the kitchen. Their contribution to the project saved ABWE thousands of dollars.

## Samuel & Lilly Wiseman

Before retiring from Caterpillar, Inc., Sam, a York County resident, had been a builder. He had previously volunteered on missionary projects in the Ivory Coast and Haiti. Hearing an announcement about ABWE's new project, he decided to volunteer his carpentry and mason skills. In an interview with York's *Daily Record,* Sam said, "I've always wanted to do something like this. I don't have any hobbies, so this is my hobby."

Sam gave more than a year of his life on the project, driving 60 round-trip miles each day. His availability and dependability impressed us all. He helped Ralph on the project right up to the end.

The Wiseman home became a refuge for the Walshes. During the course of the project they fled there from time to time for rest, fellowship, and to sample Lilly's cooking. Sam and Lilly have since served the Lord on ABWE projects in the Ukraine and Portugal, and at the Rio Grande Bible Institute in Edinburg, Texas.

## Willmer Stilwell

Will was another of those special volunteers who stuck with it for the entire length of the project. He drove in from the state of Washington with a used Toyota pickup crammed full of tools (and a space where he could curl up and sleep when he was tired of driving). Will came aboard as the carpenter superintendent and never missed a day except during the 1993 "storm of the century." Even then, when nobody else even thought of leaving home, Will and his helper, Pete Hollander, managed to get up the hill. After working a couple of hours in the flying snow, they decided to leave if they were to make it home at all. We shoveled and pushed them out of the parking lot to a point where gravity took over and helped them down the hill.

Before Will left the mountain for his home in Seattle he "willed" his old pickup to ABWE for errands around the mission. The Lord made it possible for him to have a "new" used Toyota that looked more likely to make it back to Washington.

## Authur & Marie Eshleman

One Sunday a lady from the Grace Baptist Church of Binghamton, New York, brought home one of Ralph's volunteer application forms and gave it to Art, who tucked it under a pile of papers on his desk and forgot about it. In the spring of 1992 he uncluttered his desk and rediscovered it. Art filled out the form and sent it to Ralph, and the rest of the story is history. Art put in 24 weeks on the project, returning time and again to share his many skills. When Eleanor asked about his wife, he said that she would love to come but couldn't be on her feet for long periods. "She can sit and cut vegetables," Eleanor challenged. That's how Marie got involved, and what a blessing she was to the kitchen crew.

When asked how the project affected him, Art replied, "It filled a dry spell in my life. I wanted to serve the Lord with my hands." Indeed he did. He came to the hill with a general knowledge, many of the skills needed, and worked his heart out.

After leaving the ABWE project, Art started his new missionary career with gusto. He has since worked on projects in Ecuador, Hungary, Ukraine, Central African Republic, South Africa, Japan, and Portugal.

## Cornelius (Connie) & Atalene DeRuyter

Connie had already lived more than seven decades when he and Atalene arrived on the mountain with their pickup and trailer. Their first stint on the project lasted three months, and they returned again later. A professional mason, Connie lifted and placed hundreds of those heavy concrete blocks in the lower level walls of the building and the rotunda. Younger men wondered how he could put in such hard labor, but he did. Toughened by wind, weather, and hard work, Connie represented life where the rubber meets the road. What a contribution he made serving his Lord.

Atalene became a permanent part of the kitchen crew and, like Lilly, made Eleanor's task so much easier. We include her name in our nominations for the cooks' "hall of fame."

### Raymond & Elizabeth Gerow

Ray heard about the project through his pastor at Berean Baptist Church of Portage, Michigan (Will Davis, also the vice president of ABWE). He responded to Ralph's appeal by volunteering for two weeks in August 1992, and another two weeks later in the project. The first several  days he worked on miscellaneous jobs, but on August 31, 1992, Ray started driving a vibrating tractor compactor in the parking lot area. On September 2, just three days before his first volunteer stint would be over, he was working at the edge of the parking lot when, in his own words, "Suddenly the right drive wheel had nothing under it. The machine started to slip, and I decided to leap off. I temporarily lost my memory until I landed hard on some jagged rocks a short distance from the tractor."

Ray's wife, Beth, was notified, and she arrived on September 4. Ray spent the next five weeks in hospitals. He went through two major back surgeries to correct spinal and pelvic fractures at Harrisburg Hospital, and later spent time at the Mechanicsburg Rehabilitation Hospital. Jay and Eleanor visited Ray every night after work. Ray always asked Jay to pray before leaving. During those days Beth divided her time between hospital visits and helping on the kitchen crew. On October 12, Ray was flown back to Michigan to begin out-patient therapy.

Several years later, on January 13, 1997, Ray would write, "A great number of people prayed for my recovery, including the ABWE staff, project workers, missionaries around the world, and many churches that heard about me. Praise the Lord, I have progressed a long way and I now can walk with forearm crutches or a three-wheel walker. I can drive my car and a self-propelled lawn mower and snow-blower. No more can I help build mission churches or work on projects like that of ABWE. I am limited now to encouraging others in difficult situations by telling them what the Lord has done for me, and praying for them."

Ray gave more than anyone else. The mission presented this plaque to the Gerows:

*With Appreciation to RAYMOND S. & ELIZABETH GEROW*
*For Your Sacrificial Service and Labor of Love.*
*May Your Labor Be Rewarded In the Worldwide*
*Furtherance of the Gospel.*
*THE MIRACLE AT HARRISBURG*
*ABWE 1993*

# Tribute

Dear Jay and Eleanor:

None of us knew what we were getting into when we agreed to come to Harrisburg. But God was in it, and we saw His hand and goodness in more ways than even your book has space to record. We saw it in the events that swirled around us, and we saw it in the wonderful people that God kept sending our way. And I saw it in you.

*Ich bin schrachloss.* That means: I try, I grope, and still the words won't come. The words that surface are all way too puny to convey what's in my heart when I remember your ministry here in Harrisburg. Without you, the project could not have been pulled off. And God knowing that, inclined your hearts this way while you were still in Bangladesh!

THANK YOU FOR OBEYING AND SERVING AS YOU DID.

Thank you, Jay, for the way you touched so many lives and helped us on those many early mornings to better understand and appreciate missions and missionary life. Thanks for all your help on the job, too. And Eleanor, your planning, your loving labors and organization, your recipes, and your touch made the day for all of us, over all those long months.

I shall ever treasure those memories. I will miss you.

Sincerely in Christ,

Ralph Gruenberg (Phil. 1:6)

William Chilionsha  Thomas Weber  Don Kunze  Henry Morris  Scott Welsh  Matt Taylor  Will Brungard  Jack Schorsch  Nancy King

## Appendix A

# HISTORY OF THE PROPERTY

In 1917 John C. Krater and his wife, Iva, purchased the farm on which ABWE is now located. The property was covered with trees except for the lower hill area which they farmed. Their water supply came from the small mountain stream that now drains into the two fish ponds.

The old barn, silo, and corn sheds on the left as you drive up the hill were built in 1920. In addition to farming, John Krater supplied meat for a butcher shop. The Kraters lived on the property until John died in 1951 and Iva died in 1967.

One year after the Kraters purchased the farm, Edna was born. She lived with her parents until she married Roderick Mills in 1936. They built the small white house just to the left of ABWE's entrance, and continue to live there at this writing. The Mills were enthusiastic cheerleaders for ABWE's project.

Wayne Prowell bought the farm from Iva Krater in 1954. He built the ranch house and lived there until his wife passed away (Mr. Prowell died on January 31, 1998). Eventually, Dr. and Mrs. Frank Freistak purchased the original farmhouse, barn, and sheds from Wayne Prowell before the rest of the estate was sold to Mr. Michael McKinney. The Freistaks still live there. The first pond on the left of ABWE's driveway belongs to them.

Michael McKinney purchased the rest of the original acreage from Wayne Prowell in October of 1985. He built the original macadam drive and gate that enters the property from Null Road. Between 1985 and 1986 he built the Capitol

View Manor and the other buildings on the property, with the exception of the ranch house, which he remodeled and enlarged as a home for his parents. He also excavated the beautiful pond hidden behind the trees.

ABWE purchased 134.19 acres from Mr. McKinney in 1991 and a 1.91 acre roadside plot from Mr. and Mrs. Roderick Mills. The Mills property provided ABWE direct access to Route 114 (Lewisberry Road) as the Township required.

## Appendix B

# DONATIONS & CONTRIBUTIONS

From the outset of construction God evidenced His approval of the project by providing special donations of materials and services through His people. Here are some of them:

- Architectural/structural design and blueprints by Mr. Roger Petrone.
- Mr. Gary Marsh, a New York Case dealer, arranged the bulldozer, loader, and backhoe equipment rentals.
- The First Baptist Church of Belmont, New York, paid for all the diesel fuel used by the heavy equipment (bulldozers, compactors, and lifts).
- A New Jersey company donated 250 squares of roofing shingles and materials—enough for the whole project.
- Al Ehrman of Ehrman's Plumbing & Heating contributed the heating, ventilation, and air-conditioning (HVAC) design and supervision.
- A Milwaukee, Wisconsin, marble company suggested we use marble, and then donated what was used in the rotunda and elsewhere.
- The Pennsylvania Power and Light Company, in a special arrangement, contributed the Megatherm Reservoir, a $32,000 item located under the rotunda to encourage us in the creative use of off-peak power. They also provided partial rebates for 38 heat pumps used in the building.
- Mark Nelson of Nelcorp in New York contributed the electrical design and prints, most of the electrical materials, and an electrical superintendent to oversee the work.

*George Minick  Mike Knauer  Paul Williams  Tad Loffing  Tony Eckstein  R. Michael Eckstein  Dan Williams  Robert Clifton  B. Dale Sanville*

- Two pickup trucks were donated. An older model with four-wheel drive was used as a runabout on the property. Mr. & Mrs. C. John Miller of Kalamazoo, Michigan, purchased a brand-new GMC, used by Jay for pickups and deliveries around the city.
- A couple from New York donated a maintenance van for storing and carrying tools.
- R. C. Skelly, a Mechanicsburg, Pennsylvania, steel contractor and engineer, donated the steel fabrication and its erection in the buildings.
- Jon Delavan from Cincinnatus, New York, donated the use of a building crane.
- A volunteer, concerned by the onset of winter to see the chapel section closed in before Christmas, gave $20,000 cash to bring in extra contracted man-power.*
- A local mason contractor volunteered to do much of the brick veneer at a special price.
- A Michigan company provided the free use of an expensive laser level for ceiling work.
- A chlorinator was donated for the water system.
- A New Jersey nursery and landscaping company furnished their architect to design the landscape.
- One man, who wishes to remain anonymous, gave $60,000—his life savings!
- A lady wrote and said she could give only $1 a month, and did so for two years!

---

*From time to time during the construction phase of the project, Ralph hired special contractors whose expertise and resources were necessary to meet Pennsylvania building codes or to supplement volunteer skills in special situations. The splendid manner in which these contractors blended into this unusual volunteer scene is a tribute to their management flexibility.

Brian Nester  Dianna Nester  Denis Friederich  Mark Schuch  G. Scott Major  Bruce Moran  Walt Major  David Zentz  David Knaus

All of these contributions, plus the skills of 1,140 volunteers saved ABWE over $2 million. The "miracle on the hill" stands as a wonderful monument to God's goodness and to His special servants who caught the vision.

## Appendix C

# OUR PHILOSOPHY OF RELOCATION

Complete text of letter
from Wendell Kempton to ABWE Staff

***Our utmost desire is to stay together, stick together, as a family.***

History is strong in its proof that during these kinds of stresses, people and organizations face unusual attacks. They are usually authored by the evil one, and they are often a repeat of the Sanballat and Tobiah and Geshem experience found in the building program of Nehemiah. Thus, we will have to practice two basic principles: (a) There must be constant communication; (b) We must promote relationships and fellowship, getting together to answer questions and keep everyone current. This will assist us in avoiding misunderstandings.

***Our utmost desire is to support one another.***

Everyone will approach this change in different ways, since our emotional makeups are so varied. Some of our staff will not be moving, while others will. Some will feel left out. Some may go through depression, and others may be filled with anxiety and worry in not knowing how everything is going to work out. Let us enter into each other's experiences. We may need to lean on one another. Do not feel hesitant to express your feelings during these days, perhaps confidentially. Whatever the case, let us support each other.

*Our utmost desire is to encourage the planning and building committee.*

These people will be involved in investing extra time in behalf of this project. They will also be in a position where they must think creatively and objectively. Many of their decisions will affect the design, layout, and overall function of the building. The importance of this committee comes into focus when one understands that we will have to minister more effectively within this new environment. They will also be aware that their decisions will be of long tenure, affecting and influencing all who follow us in this ministry. Sensing this awesome assignment, they will need cheerleaders from time to time.

*Our utmost desire is to involve you in this process.*

We will allow everyone to share his or her ideas, concepts, desires, and concerns. The committee will meet with the various divisions within the mission and individuals to solicit input. We are zealous to have everyone involved. Each individual is important to the success of this project. This is a rare opportunity that seldom comes into our lives. May we, together, have an uninhibited, creative, common sense, inspired team effort.

*Our utmost desire is to strive to be good stewards.*

This stewardship will involve our time, our investment, our space allocation, and our costs for the total project. These next 21 months will fly by. Every week will be very important. How we use time will be crucial. All the days must be counted and the planning of minor and major events, the sequence of those happenings, and the flow. Each day is a link that ties into another. They all have to be in order, and they will finally end up being that inseparable chain. Perhaps this is something of what the wise man was saying when he wrote: "Prepare your outside work. Make it fit for yourself in the field, and afterwards build your house" (Proverbs 24:27).

The proper use of space is also of great importance. Since we may be more aware of this science now than when we built in Cherry Hill, we will give this our careful attention. The design and layout of the building is key. It will be wise for the committee to sit with several consultants. This should not hinder or curb individuals, departments, and the committee in their aspirations or even dreams. We must be free to think big, think small, think wisely, and think objectively. Our goal is to end up with a facility that is more functional. It must result in a design and layout that seeks to maximize every inch of space. This may mean a smaller building. It may mean a larger one. Smaller space does not necessarily mean restriction and confinement. Larger space does not guarantee proper use of space or even expansion. The rooms can only be divided and subdivided in so many ways. Everyone will be confronted with big decisions. It is for this reason that the decisions must be good ones, ones that can be justified and lined up with previous decisions and those that will follow.

There is also stewardship of dollars. At this writing there are only estimates as to what will be the total cost of this project. We will monitor and be careful to watch every expenditure. This will take time as comparisons will be made prior to purchases of all material. We will strive to build with the very best material and for the best price. Our goal will be to do things right.

Presently commercial builders tell us that we can build in the Harrisburg area for $65.00 per square foot. There will be other substantial expenditures such as the construction of a road into the property. Unexpected costs are always part of any project. This all adds up to big dollars. I am sure that God has given us the kind of leadership that will insure the board, staff, missionary family, and donors of a job well done, and all within the framework of a budget.

*Patti Haller  Barbara Jackson  Dan Branda  Doug Gossel  Harold Gossel  Beth Trott  Natalie Beck  Traci Turner  Pat Henry  Bob Henry*

***Our utmost desire is to build much of the new
building with volunteer help.***

Most people tell us that this cannot be done during this
hour of history. My response is, "You may be right, but we are
going to do it." We desire to use craftsmen who will volunteer
a week of their vacation time assisting us with the project. We
will have to carefully plan each event so that the specified
laborers are present. Churches will have to be enlisted.
Pastors will have to promote this among their people.
Churches and pastors will make a commitment to this project
and principle. From their congregations they will send gifted
and willing servants. If the Amish can raise up a house or barn
and if the Jehovah's Witnesses can build their headquarters
building with volunteer labor, then our churches can also
enter into such with all their hearts. We, too, are committed to
the principle of volunteerism. This is how the bulk of the labor
will be done.

I have already contacted several churches and individuals. These pastors and lay people are excited about the
prospects, and have pledged to be involved. They also com-
mend us regarding our approach to the building program;
it will be a big undertaking, but it will be rewarding. Our
entire ABWE family will be able to declare once again the
awesome goodness and greatness of God as we involve many
people, and save money.

***Our utmost desire will be to practice patience
and perseverance.***

This will have to be the plural possessive kind, as we enter
individually and corporately into this experience. Whether we
intend to stay in this area or move, patience and perseverance
must prevail. These inseparable twins can be burdensome,
as some things take longer than anticipated.  Smooth sailing
has never accompanied any relocation or building program.

There will be differences of opinion. Thus, the heralded cry is to be patient with one another, and persevere!

**_Our utmost desire is to maintain a good attitude._**

Even though you may not be on the front lines, keep a good attitude. Though others may be the decision-makers, keep a good spirit. When the committee chooses not to take your counsel, suggestion, or desire, maintain a positive position. When members of the planning committee are working through differences, hold tight to a proper attitude.

There are ten commandments for those who are on the move, and for those who will stay. Moses received his commandments on top of a mountain; I received mine while traveling on an airplane bound for Cleveland. His were divine; mine are not. Nevertheless, there is some significance and importance in this listing. It reads easy and practices hard, especially during the stressful times and days ahead of us.

1) Thou shalt not have a critical spirit. (I would never do it that way. They are not sincere. Everything is political.)
2) Thou shalt not have a pessimistic spirit. (It won't happen; it never has.)
3) Thou shalt not have a caustic spirit. (I'm going to tell them a thing or two.)
4) Thou shalt not have a foreboding spirit. (I knew something bad would happen. I predicted it.)
5) Thou shalt not have a superior spirit. (I can do it better.)
6) Thou shalt not have a dominant spirit. (I'll take charge and have the last word.)
7) Thou shalt not have a pouting spirit. (I didn't get my way so I'm going to take a long walk. Who knows; I may not come back.)
8) Thou shalt not have an unforgiving spirit. (He hurt me. She is out to get me. I'll get even. I'll never forget what happened.)

9) Thou shalt not have a tired spirit. (I'll never get it all done. I really don't enjoy it any more.)

10) Daily protect and promote a beautiful spirit, and thou shalt be blessed and honored of the Lord. (In everything I will give thanks. I'm going to practice the presence of the Lord.)

### *Our utmost desire is to strive for excellence.*

Our goal is excellence throughout the project: in the myriad of details, in relationships, and in decisions. Perhaps it would be good to define this excellence, "doing the very best we can in all we do, in order to serve others and to exalt and honor the Lord."

### *Our utmost desire is to move through every step with a prayerful spirit.*

We will need much more than we have, much more than we are, and much more than any consultant can share. Our best position in the future will be that of a child. At our best we know very little, have little to offer, and are incapable of the task before us. Even if we have gathered experience in our past, we dare not lean too heavily upon it. We must always pray. This will take time, but God honors those who are as little children. Honest humility is one of the greatest qualities we can take as we pursue our goals. No one in world history has ever traveled down this road before. God has set this one out for us. We cannot improve upon: "Trust in the Lord with all thine heart; and lean not unto thine own understanding. In all thy ways acknowledge Him, and He shall direct thy paths" (Proverbs 3:5,6).

Prayer must preface, prevail, and follow every aspect of our venture of faith. It is prayer that will give us discernment and wisdom. It will be prayer that will keep us quiet, content, and full of faith. Prayer will strengthen those who are left behind. Prayer will sell our homes and sell our present property.

It will guide us in the timing of all these important events. Intercession will help all of us with our patience and perseverance. Prayer will help us stay together (though some will depart), support one another, assist us as we move through transition, find other good jobs, and enable us to give thanks in all things. It will help us to be like Christ. Prayer will make this new road a bright and shining path in our life and mission experience.

**_Finally, our philosophy is to sincerely desire to honor those who stay behind._**

We have made a thorough investigation of four mission agencies that have preceded us in relocation. One of those organizations followed a procedure which we felt was honorable and practical, and we will follow their example. All employees of ABWE who will not be making the move will be encouraged to stay right to the very end. We know the value of keeping our team together, yet those who stay must think wisely of their future. Some of the questions include: Where will I work? When is the right time for me to be seeking another job?

All of these questions are justified and must be answered to your satisfaction. We desire to be understanding and helpful; thus, the administration has committed itself to allowing all full-time people, according to your time schedule, to interview for other possible job opportunities any time during the three months prior to our departure. This can be done without penalizing your time or pay. You should work this out with your department head and the personnel director. However, for those full-time people who can make a complete commitment to the very end, who can time your departure in concert with ours, we will give you three months of pay. This can be accepted as a bonus, or it can financially assist you as you seek other employment. It is our way of helping you because of your assistance to ABWE. And for those who have eight years of service, ABWE will permit an early payout or rollover of your future retirement benefits as calculated and approved by the Finance Committee. This is the best way we can be fair to you and to the mission.

To those who stay, may our God watch over you in special ways. We will support you with our love and prayers. God will go before you as the Shepherd, preparing the way and watching over all your future needs. The departure is still 21 months away, but some of us already feel the pain of separation. For those who stay, it will not be easy, and for those who uproot, the changes may be even more traumatic.

All of this is rather scary. None of us has taken enough courses on properly handling the unknown. For most of us the unknown confronts us with darkness. It sensitizes our emotions and captures our imaginations. We wonder how will it all work out. We think it is coming at the wrong time of our lives. I sure hope Kempton knows what he is doing. Charting unknown waters can strike fear into our minds and hearts. It can make us reluctant to enter the boat for the journey. It is great to be intimately acquainted with the One who calms storms and walks on water. He will be walking along our side and even be in our boat. The Shepherd is experienced in leading His sheep to other fields, as well as taking us through uncharted waters. *Lead On, O King Eternal.* May You be honored and glorified through it all.

*Sarah Edsell  Scotte Staab  Beth Ann Staab  Lori Haskell  Brenda Holder  Debbie Johnson  Janice Kunze*